James

Maturing in Faith

Name _____

James

Maturing in Faith

Five Day Format

Each lesson is broken down into five separate days. This is only a recommended way to divide your study. A woman may use this breakdown or another of her choosing.

Memory Verse

Each lesson will include a memory verse on page 2. The memory verse should be learned for the week the lesson is discussed in your group.

Digging Deeper

For further study into the book of James, give the section titled "Digging Deeper" a try.

James, Maturing in Faith
Copyright © 2014 by Salem Heights Church Women's Ministries
All rights reserved.

Scripture taken from the NEW AMERICAN STANDARD BIBLE®

Copyright©1960, 1962, 1963, 1968, 1971, 1972, 1973, 1975, 1977, 1995
by The Lockman Foundation. Used by permission.

All artwork is used by permission. All rights reserved.

Contributing Authors

James, Maturing in Faith

Emily Dempster is serving as the Curriculum Coordinator for Salem Heights Church Women's Ministries. She earned her Masters in Pastoral Counseling through Liberty Theological Seminary University. She has a passion for discipleship in the church and seeing women's lives changed as a result of God's Word. When given the chance, Emily loves skiing, hiking and fishing in Central Oregon with her husband and two children.

Julie Bernard serves as the Women's Ministry Director at Salem Heights Church. She loves the team approach to ministry and encouraging and developing Women's Ministry leaders. She enjoys drinking coffee with friends, snuggling with her four grandchildren, and golfing with her husband.

Tara Cox currently serves as the Girls' Night Out Coordinator for Salem Heights Church Women's Ministry. She graduated from Corban University with a B.S. in Biblical Studies and is hoping to complete her Master's Degree. She spends most of her time chasing, dancing, reading to and otherwise growing up her three girls alongside her husband. She has a passion to see others come to know and love God through the study of His Word.

Celeste Starr is a wife and a mom. She enjoys leading small groups of women in discipleship, learning more about God's Word and volunteering for various women's ministries. Celeste and her family enjoy going on many adventures that take them out into the world to marvel at the wonders that God has created.

Rebecca Griffiths loves to study God's Word and witness how the lives of women are impacted as they interact with God and His truth. She is a wife and mom of two boys, and serves as a leader in the Salem Heights Church Discipleship program. Rebecca and her family love nature and enjoy the beautiful state of Oregon by way of hiking, canoeing, camping, or backpacking.

Julie McGinty is a retired R.N. who has taught piano in her home for over forty years. She loves delving into intensive personal Bible study, as well as encouraging other women to do the same by serving as a facilitator for Women's Discipleship Studies. Julie loves serving on her church Music Team, spending time with her grandchildren, and aerobic walking.

Pam Williams has a degree in Psychology from Corban University and is currently involved in Biblical Counseling/Mentoring at Salem Heights Church as well as www.settingcaptivesfree.com. Her passion is to not only see marriages healed and restored, but to encourage women to be diligently practicing what they know to be true from God's Word. Pam is married and has three daughters and one son-in-law. She loves camping, biking and hiking with them. After taking eighteen years off to raise her daughters, she is back to work as an instructional assistant with special needs children.

Cindy Helsley enjoys teaching Sunday school alongside her husband at Salem Heights Church. She and a friend are also leading a small group of tennis buddies through the book of John. She was saved as a teenager, but fell into a religious lifestyle of do's and don'ts. After getting involved in a deep study of God's Word, she realized that God didn't want her outward allegiance only. She learned that God wanted a special relationship, with a transformation that occurred from the inside out. In her free time, she enjoys crafting, decorating and playing tennis.

Karin Penn considers herself a Californegonian since settling in Oregon after college. She has been deeply impacted by the teaching at Salem Heights Church and loves attending there with her husband and two boys. She loves to crack a good joke and make people laugh. She feels privileged to have been able to serve in Women's Ministries for almost twenty years.

Other Contributors - *Lauren Bain, Lauren Bernard, Jenn Elliott, Angi Greene, DeAnna Jones, Sally Lewin, Stacey Moore, Lynn Piper, Erin Rowzee, Sue Saffeels, Gina Weigand*

Table of Contents
James, Maturing in Faith

Lesson 1	Introduction	1-1
Lesson 2	Rejoice in Trials, Part 1	2-1
Lesson 3	Rejoice in Trials, Part 2	3-1
Lesson 4	Rejoice in Trials, Part 3	4-1
Lesson 5	Do Not Blame God	5-1
Lesson 6	Respond Correctly to God's Perfect Gifts	6-1
Lesson 7	Respond Correctly to God's Word	7-1
Lesson 8	Do Not Show Favoritism, Part 1	8-1
Lesson 9	Do Not Show Favoritism, Part 2	9-1
Lesson 10	Show Faith Through Works	10-1
Lesson 11	Take Action	11-1
Lesson 12	Control Your Tongue, Part 1	12-1
Lesson 13	Control Your Tongue, Part 2	13-1
Lesson 14	Exhibit Godly Wisdom	14-1
Lesson 15	Have a Heart Focused on God	15-1
Lesson 16	Have a Humble Heart	16-1
Lesson 17	Give Grace	17-1
Lesson 18	Trust God's Will	18-1
Lesson 19	Use Riches in a Godly Way	19-1
Lesson 20	Display Patient Endurance in the Midst of Suffering	20-1
Lesson 21	Pray Earnestly and Effectively	21-1
Lesson 22	A Final Evaluation	22-1

Lesson One

Introduction

James, Maturing in Faith

Recently, a friend attending a dinner party was asked to make her signature dessert. Everyone had either experienced it before or had heard rave reviews. She brought her basket of ingredients to the home of the host so that she could make it there and serve it right out of the oven after dinner. Because it was a housewarming party, the oven had yet to be used by the new homeowner. Like her grandmother had taught her in her first baking lesson, she poked a toothpick into the center to check for doneness at the sound of the timer. It wasn't done. She lowered the temp slightly and gave it another five minutes. Still, no. One more decrease and five more minutes seemed to do the trick, but when she began to serve her masterpiece, she could see that it had burned on the bottom. Thankfully, Grandma had also taught her the art of disguise. She quickly sliced off the offending portion and set each serving atop a swirl of chocolate and caramel sauces.

The host would never tell her secret and made an appointment to have the oven correctly calibrated the next day. She knew that the toothpick never lies, but sometimes an unchecked thermometer might just try.

As reliable as a toothpick, the book of James evaluates the reality of faith. It was written to Christian Jews, some that had been present at the day of Pentecost. Returning home, they brought with them the truth that Christ was the Messiah, the one who was crucified, buried and raised from the dead. Knowing little more than that, they returned to the synagogues, some thinking it was necessary to keep the Law. Caught between Law and grace, they quickly found they were no longer accepted by the Jews *or* the Greeks. Forced out, they scattered throughout Palestine and Asia Minor.

James takes this opportunity to write a letter of encouragement to both the early believers and to us! Simply and clearly, he describes what belief in the gospel of grace looks like in real life.

Much like a baker pokes a toothpick into the middle of a cake to test if it is done, James encourages believers to evaluate their actions and consider where their faith can mature.

Day One
What Do I See?

In each of our lessons, the first day of study will be entitled "What Do I See?" Basic observations are made to gain an understanding of the passage and build personal Bible study skills. The first day will end with a "Prepare Your Heart" section to get our hearts ready for what the Lord will show us in this study.

In this first lesson we will be getting the "big picture" of the book of James. You may feel like you want to investigate details as you go through this lesson, but it is important to get an overview of the book first. Each day this week we will read through the entire book of James like a letter, just like it was written to you. On at least one of the days, try reading it aloud to yourself, reading it to someone else, or listening to it on Biblegateway.com.

1. **Describe a time when you had a letter of encouragement written to you. Why was it encouraging?**

2. **Read James. As you read, make some basic observations. Make notes of words you might not understand, ideas you want to know more about, and questions you may have.**

3. **After reading James, what title would you give the book?**

Memory Verse

"But prove yourselves doers of the word, and not merely hearers who delude themselves."

James 1:22

PREPARE YOUR HEART {♥}

4. What are your initial thoughts as you read James today?

5. What are you hoping to gain from this study?

6. Be still before the Lord. Ask the Holy Spirit to teach, mature, and guide you this week.

Day Two
Who Is James?

As we continue to gather the "big picture" of James, we will record everything we have learned about the author of this book.

7. Read James. What did you learn about the author James? Write observations and words related to him there.

8. Why did he write this book?

9. Look up the following Scriptures to find out more about James.

    Matthew 13:53-55

    Mark 6:3

    1 Corinthians 15:3-7

    Galatians 2:9

Although a popular name at the time, most scholars agree that the author of the book of James is the half-brother of Jesus.

10. In James 1:1, James calls himself a bond-servant. Look at the definition of the word *bond-servant* in the sidebar. How does the way in which James addresses himself make you think about James as a person?

11. What examples from your own life show that you are a bond-servant of Christ?

Day Three
Who Are the Readers?

Continue to *explore* the book of James by reading the entire book again. Today, we will focus on who the readers of this book are.

12. Read James. As you read today, jot down any phrases or words that give you clues as to who the readers are. What specific names did James call them?

13. What additional information can you find from your study Bible or a commentary about the readers of this letter?

14. Look up "dispersed" in the dictionary or at hyperdictionary.com. What did you find?

15. What were some of the possible reasons the readers were "dispersed" abroad (see introduction; Deuteronomy 4:25-28; Acts 8:1)? How might they feel?

16. What did God impress upon *you* as you read James today?

Key Terms

Bond-servant: "To bind, a slave, originally the lowest term in the scale of servitude; who gives himself up to the will of another."[xi]

Twelve Tribes: A term used in James's day to include all Jewish Christians outside Palestine.

1-4

Day Four

Why Did James Write This Letter?

17. Nature lovers will enjoy the book of James as he uses many examples in his writing. Read James and use the chart below to record examples from nature and what they explain.

EXAMPLE OF NATURE	WHAT THE NATURE REFERENCE EXPLAINS

What was your favorite example? How has God used it to minister to your heart?

18. To better understand why James wrote the book, summarize the following verses:

    James 1:2-4

    James 1:17

    James 2:18-20

    James 3:6

    James 3:17

    James 4:6-7

    James 5:16

Notes

1-5

Day Five
What Did We Learn from James?

Can you believe what we have learned so far through this investigation? In the lessons that follow, we will identify several aspects of faith and examples of it from people in Scripture. Today, as we read through James one last time, let's start by seeing how many characteristics we can discover on our own (no peeking ahead).

19. Read James and complete the chart below.

ASPECT OF FAITH	VERSE

Which characteristic are you looking forward to exploring more? Why?

20. After studying the big picture of James this week, how would you revise your title for the book (Day 1, #3)?

21. As you study James this year, what do you hope God will do in your life?

Notes

Lesson Two

Rejoice in Trials, Part 1

James 1:1-4

Beth was a lifelong walker and found many items of value over the years. She mostly found coins, but an occasional dollar bill and even a couple of fives had been known to cross her path. There was the one-time find of a twenty dollar bill lying next to the sidewalk. Seeing no one around to claim it, she did! *It pays to look down now and then when you're walking*, she thought. A red garnet ring and a cloisonné thimble were two of her all-time favorite finds. Efforts to find the owners proved fruitless. She wondered if any of the items she had lost over the years had made other people happy.

While walking through the giant redwoods in a local park early one morning, Beth came upon a wallet. She thought the name and picture on the driver's license seemed a little familiar, but couldn't place the man. When she got home and showed her son the wallet, he exclaimed, "That's my teacher!" After contact had been made, a very grateful middle school teacher showed up to claim his wallet. Evidently, it had fallen out of his pocket on a bike ride.

Early one Thanksgiving morning, Beth put the large turkey in the oven and took off for her walk. It seemed most of the city, as well as her family, was still asleep. After walking several blocks she discovered a black eel skin wallet lying in the street. It contained a large amount of cash as well as several credit cards. *Surely the owner must be frantic*, she thought. The driver's license revealed the owner to be a twenty-year-old woman who lived several miles from this location. Beth returned home and located the young woman's number in the phone book. When the call was made, and the owner informed that her wallet had been found intact, she expressed surprise rather than relief. She hadn't even missed it yet! She had apparently dropped it while visiting with friends in that neighborhood after Christmas shopping. Her gratitude at the wallet's return was minimal, at best. She had simply not considered the ramifications of a dishonest person finding it.

The extreme relief and gratitude expressed by the teacher certainly contrasted with the response of the young woman. Both incidents caused Beth to thank God for His grace in the times trials were quickly resolved, as well as when they were obviously, and narrowly, averted in her life.

We all have trials. Jesus said we would. But whether long term with no end in sight, or short term and quickly resolved, James tells us how to deal with them in a manner that reflects our faith.

Day One
What Do I See?

1. Share a time when you experienced the return of a treasured lost item.

Read James 1:1-12

James 1:2-4

²Consider it all joy, my brethren, when you encounter various trials,
³knowing that the testing of your faith produces endurance.
⁴And let endurance have its perfect result, so that you may be perfect and complete, lacking in nothing.

2. Put a box around James's instruction.

3. Circle the results from that instruction.

4. Underline the terms you see that identify the process leading to that outcome.

PREPARE YOUR HEART {♥}

5. James says to be "doers of the word not merely hearers." In every lesson we will ask: What result of genuine faith is identified in this passage? In other words, if you are growing in the Lord and not only hearing the Word, what would you be doing? What is displayed in your actions? Answer this question for James 1:2-4.

6. What are your initial thoughts about these truths?

7. Be still before the Lord. Ask the Holy Spirit to teach, mature, and guide you this week.

Memory Verse

"Consider it all joy, my brethren, when you encounter various trials, knowing that the testing of your faith produces endurance. And let endurance have its perfect result, so that you may be perfect and complete, lacking in nothing."

James 1:2-4

Day Two
The Proper Response to Trials

> Read James 1:2-4

The Greek word for "face" or "encounter" is *peripipto* (verse two) and suggests an unwelcome and unanticipated experience, as "falling into" a situation. Jesus used the same word when He related the story of the Good Samaritan who "fell among thieves" (KJV, Luke 10:30).

8. How might James's instruction be interpreted as seemingly "unreasonable"?

   What is a "natural" response to trials?

James has in mind a situation of testing through trouble that is caused by any sort of hardship, problem, or difficulty. Trials are the common experience of mankind, including Jesus.

9. Read the following verses, then examine and record the various emotions Jesus experienced as He faced His own trial.

   Matthew 26:36-42

   Luke 12:49-50; John 12:27

   Hebrews 12:2-3

   How do His responses encourage you?

10. What kind of joy are we to experience when faced with a trial? Explain.

    What does our response indicate about our spiritual condition?

11. Re-read James 1:3. What does James say we *know*?

    How can this knowledge change our attitude when trials come?

"Knowing" in Scripture is more than just intellectual perception; it is something gained through daily experience in life. One commentator states that everyone has experienced both the pain of problems and the resulting profit of persistence.

12. Are you currently finding it "unreasonable" to rejoice *in* (not *for*, Romans 5:3) a personal trial? Consider what you know to be true as you ask God for wisdom, peace, understanding, and joy (Romans 8:28). Write a prayer to God expressing the difficulty you're having in finding reasons to rejoice in current circumstances, and invite Him to take control.

Day Three
The Advantage of Trials

Read James 1:2-4

13. What phrase used in verse 2 is telling us to expect trials in our lives? How does this awareness affect you spiritually on a daily basis?

"The Gospels generally see maturity as the imitation of God, the development of the character traits of God within ourselves."[1]

The term "various trials" (NASB) or "trials of many kinds" (NIV) indicates that a great variety of trials, literally "variegated" or "many-colored," may come upon the believer. Our trials will come in many shapes, shades, and degrees, and they test our faith. A good reminder is that God's grace is sufficient for every trial no matter the color (2 Corinthians 12:9).

14. List the types of trials that have affected you or others known to you.

Reflect on the outcome of past trials. Share how you have seen God at work when He was called alongside to help.

15. Read the following verses and record the reasons God allowed tests to take place.

Genesis 22:12

Exodus 16:4

Exodus 20:20

Deuteronomy 8:2, 16

Job 23:10

1 Peter 1:6-7

The testing of our faith proves we are saved.

In Scripture, testing most often leads to a good end. It causes the person being tested to emerge stronger and better, in loyalty and faith. The testing of our faith proves we are saved. James was telling his readers that the trials they were undergoing were in the permissive will of God to prove the maturity of their faith.

16. Record the definitions for *perseverance* and *patience*.

Explain the difference between the two.

17. How do your answers encourage you as you persevere in difficult circumstances, with patience?

DIGGING DEEPER

Mature, perfect, and complete are words often used interchangeably in Scripture. Read the following verses and record the various aspects of Christian maturity.

Matthew 5:48

Luke 8:14

1 Corinthians 14:20

Ephesians 4:13

Colossians 1:28

Hebrews 5:13-14

Summarize the meaning of Christian maturity.

Key Term

Testing: The Greek term *dokimion* means "approved character." It indicates the testing of something in order to prove or disprove its validity or genuineness, as in the assaying of gold or silver for purity. The verb would also be used, for example, of a young bird "testing" its wings, or the "testing" of drugs to see if they would be effective in curing diseases.

Day Four
Paul's Faith

> Read James 1:2-4

One commentator noted that Paul the Apostle was unique, stating that "no man in the history of the Christian Church has been more unflagging in Christian toil and zeal."[2]

> Read 2 Corinthians 11:16-33

This is Paul's own summary of his trials and sufferings over the course of his ministry. In this portion of Scripture, he is awkwardly "boasting" of his experiences in order to challenge his opponents, false apostles who had invaded the church at Corinth, meeting them on their own ground.

18. Identify key thoughts from each verse and how they can encourage you in trials.

VERSE	KEY THOUGHTS	ENCOURAGEMENT IN TRIALS
Romans 5:3-4		
Romans 15:4		
2 Corinthians 4:16-18		
2 Corinthians 12:7-10		

2-7

19. Read Philippians 4:11-13. What did Paul learn, and what was the "secret" he found?

20. Read Philippians 3:12-14. What was Paul's ambition?

    Prayerfully consider what you may need to leave behind in order to press forward.

21. How do Paul's attitudes and responses to trials compare to those of James?

Day Five
STEPPING UP TO MATURITY

> Read James 1:2-4

22. Find an example in Scripture of a person who did not respond with faith when tested. How did their actions affect others? What did their life reveal about their faith in God? What could they have done differently to follow what James is teaching in this passage? What can you learn from this example?

23. Consider your response when trials and troubles come. Are you able to rejoice as James instructs us? Why or why not?

24. Review what you have learned this week about *the purpose and result of trials*. Write a principle for living a life of faith based on this passage.

25. What step(s) will you take this week to be a *doer of the Word and not a hearer only* (James 1:22)?

Notes

2-9

Lesson Three

Rejoice in Trials, Part 2

James 1:5-8

Nick and Carli were thrilled that Nick's request for a job transfer to another part of the state had been granted. The young couple was looking forward to living in a smaller community, away from the hustle and bustle of the large city where they currently lived. They felt it would be a better place to raise their children, three-year-old Natalie and two-year-old Josh.

Moving boxes and clutter seemed to overwhelm the tiny house. The movers would be there the next day to pack up their belongings. Taking advantage of the kids' naptime, Nick and Carli were busily finishing up the loading, labeling, and securing of the multiple boxes. They wondered audibly how they'd managed to accumulate so much "stuff" in only seven years of marriage.

Suddenly, they heard Natalie's panic-stricken scream, "Mommy ... Daddy...!" They ran to her bedroom and saw her empty bed. The screams continued. Now thinking the cries were coming from the backyard, they ran through the house in that direction. Scanning the backyard from the porch, further screams indicated Natalie was in the house ... but where? They ran back and forth, becoming panic-stricken themselves, unable to determine the location of their terrified, precious daughter. In a searching frenzy, they were obviously passing her location time and time again. Where could she be? Carli's eyes fell on the emptied, unplugged refrigerator. When she opened its door, a sobbing little girl fell into her arms. What a tearful and joyful reunion the three of them had. Natalie had thought that would be a good place to hide. Josh slept through it all!

God invites us to cry out for His help, to ask for His wisdom in maneuvering through hard times, no matter the origin. He promises to answer our pleas for help.

Day One
What Do I See?

1. Have you ever had an experience when you cried out for help, or responded to another's cry for help, in a desperate situation? Share your experience.

> Read James 1:1-12

James 1:5-8

⁵But if any of you lacks wisdom, let him ask of God, who gives to all generously and without reproach, and it will be given to him.
⁶But he must ask in faith without any doubting, for the one who doubts is like the surf of the sea, driven and tossed by the wind.
⁷For that man ought not to expect that he will receive anything from the Lord,
⁸being a double-minded man, unstable in all his ways.

2. Underline the key words and phrases from this passage, and record your thoughts on the meaning of each.

3. What issues does James address in these verses?

4. What do you learn is necessary for answered prayer?

PREPARE YOUR HEART {♥}

5. What result of genuine faith is identified in this passage?

6. What are your initial thoughts about these truths?

7. Be still before the Lord. Ask the Holy Spirit to teach, mature, and guide you this week.

Memory Verse

"But if any of you lacks wisdom, let him ask of God, who gives to all generously and without reproach, and it will be given to him."

James 1:5

Day Two
Assistance in Trials

> Read James 1:5-8

8. What should we ask for when going through difficulties? How are we to ask, and why?

9. From verse five, describe God's responses to our requests. How does His response impact you?

10. Read Hebrews 4:14-16. What assurance do you find in this passage of our access to God? Which aspect is most meaningful to you?

11. Using a dictionary, find and record the definitions of both *knowledge* and *wisdom*. In your own words explain the difference between the two.

    Knowledge is knowing that tomato is fruit. Wisdom is knowing not to add it to your fruit salad.

12. How would you respond to a college professor who would tell you that the thought of a God who you can talk with, actually answers, and cares about the world is foolish?

DIGGING DEEPER

The type of wisdom we lack and are to ask for is the kind that plays such a large part in the book of Proverbs. Wisdom must come from God. It is not automatic, however, but requires diligent searching.

Read Proverbs 2. What benefits of finding and applying wisdom do you find in this chapter?

Wisdom must come from God. It is not automatic, however, but requires diligent searching.

13. We need wisdom so we will not waste the opportunity God is giving us to mature, and ultimately understand how to use trials for our good and God's glory. What trial will you give over to Him right now? Ask Him for the strength and wisdom you need to see you through it.

Day Three
Prerequisites of Answered Prayer

Read James 1:5-8

14. What important conditions are necessary for effective prayer? List the conditions you find in the following verses.

    Mark 11:22-24

    John 14:13-14

    1 John 3:21-22

    1 John 5:14-15

3-4

MOSES' FAITH

Moses was God's chosen man to lead His children out of Egypt to the Promised Land. After offering God multiple excuses as to why he should NOT be the chosen man, Moses allowed God to change and use him in a history-changing way. He became a man of faith. Moses chose "rather to endure ill-treatment with the people of God than to enjoy the passing pleasures of sin" (Hebrews 11:25). He considered "the reproach of Christ greater riches than the treasures of Egypt; for he was looking to the reward" (Hebrews 11:26).

In each crisis in the desert, Moses asked for God's direction and wisdom to know what to do, and each time we read that he was given that wisdom when he needed it.

15. From the following Scriptures in the chart below, record the evidence of Moses' faith.

VERSES	LOCATION	CRISIS	GOD'S INSTRUCTION AND RESPONSE
Exodus 14:9-10, 13-16			
Exodus 15:22-25			
Exodus 16:1-4			
Exodus 17:1-6			
Exodus 17:8-16			

Notes

16. What differences do you see between the attitudes of the Israelites and those of Moses?

17. Of what did Moses remind the people about their complaining in Exodus 16:7-8?

18. Have you been mumbling and grumbling over a current trial? Have you forgotten that testing is a necessary part of our earthly journey as we travel to our Promised Land? Make a list of ways God has been faithful, and praise Him for His faithfulness.

Day Four
Ask Without Doubting

Read James 1:5-8

19. How does verse six say we are to pray? Fill in the blanks:

    ASK IN _____ WITHOUT ANY _____.

20. James does not have in mind here the honest intellectual doubts that affect all believers at times. Examine the following Scriptures and summarize the doubts exhibited.

    Matthew 14:25-31

    Mark 9:17-24

    Luke 17:5-6

Notes

To the Hebrew people, the metaphor of a rough sea is symbolic of evil and uncertainty. James is trying to convey the point that the doubter is uncertain and unstable. He uses the term, "double-minded" which suggests the state of having a divided mind, being double-hearted (Psalm 12:2) and torn in two directions. One soul is turned Godward, the other toward the world. One believes God, the other disbelieves. In *Pilgrim's Progress*, John Bunyan calls such a man "Mister Facing Both Ways." That is, of course, physically impossible, and just as impossible spiritually.

21. **Read 1 Kings 18:21 and record how Elijah challenged the double-minded Israelites. Read the same verse in other Bible versions and list the terms you find for their double-mindedness.**

"One who doubts" (verse six) suggests not so much *weakness* of faith, but *lack* of it. This person is a habitual doubter, regularly praying without faith, and is compared to a wind-whipped wave. Until the risen Christ appeared before him, James himself had been a doubter concerning his brother's Messianic claims. He well understood the nature of doubting.

22. **What can one who prays with doubt expect from the Lord? Explain your thoughts.**

23. **How does habitual doubt make a person "unstable in all his ways"?**

24. **Knowing that faith is a critical element of answered prayer, how would you characterize your prayer life?**

25. **The father in Mark 9:24 was not a double-minded man wavering between belief and unbelief. He wanted to believe and felt the inadequacy of his faith, asking for help in believing. Examine your own heart. Have you allowed doubt to creep in and undermine your faith? Ask God to help you set your heart to believe.**

Notes

Day Five
STEPPING UP TO MATURITY

Read James 1:5-8

26. Find an example in Scripture of a person who trusted God's will for their plans. How did their actions affect others? What did their life reveal about their faith in God? What can you learn from this example?

27. Review what you have discovered about *praying with faith* this week. Write a principle for living a life of faith based on this passage.

28. What step(s) will you take this week to be a *doer of the Word and not a hearer only* (James 1:22)?

Notes

Lesson Four

Rejoice in Trials, Part 3

James 1:9-12

The group of backpackers from the church eagerly looked forward to their annual summer trek. Generally, ten to fifteen hikers hit the trail in the beautiful Marble Mountains of northern California.

Their experienced leader, Dennis, was an avid outdoorsman who was familiar with the great expanse of the region, having led mutiple fifty-mile Boy Scout hikes in the area. The group trusted him to choose their route and destination, which always offered ample opportunity to revel in God's beautiful creation. The shared experiences from the trips deepened friendships and fellowship over the years. This year was to be no exception.

Usually on one of the days of the adventure, about half of the group planned a day-hike while the rest stayed back at the base camp to swim, fish, relax or the like. Saturday morning arrived and the intrepid group was ready to go. "This is our destination," Dennis said, pointing to the location on the backpack guide map. It looked to be a great hike, ending at a high elevation affording a prime vantage point from which to view Mt. Shasta. Compass in hand, Dennis soon led the energized hikers on their way. After several hours of trekking, climbing, descending, slipping into gullies, and several starts and stops of thwarted routes, they had not yet reached their desired destination. They stopped to rest and discuss options. The intrepid group didn't feel so intrepid anymore. Dennis decided to check the guidebook, which he apparently hadn't checked before, figuring he knew the way. The guidebook instructs hikers how to get from one specific point to another. This is what the book stated regarding the best route from their base camp to their desired location: "YOU'RE ON YOUR OWN!" That would have been valuable information to have had ahead of time.

As foolish as it seems to take off on a hike without directions, many people navigate through life that way. We have a Guidebook, the Bible, which offers wise instruction on how to navigate through this temporary journey on earth. James offers some insight on the matter.

Day One
What Do I See?

1. Recall a time you were lost. What happened?

> Read James 1:1-12

James 1:9-12

⁹But the brother of humble circumstances is to glory in his high position;
¹⁰and the rich man is to glory in his humiliation, because like flowering grass he will pass away.
¹¹For the sun rises with a scorching wind and withers the grass; and its flower falls off and the beauty of its appearance is destroyed; so too the rich man in the midst of his pursuits will fade away.
¹²Blessed is a man who perseveres under trial; for once he has been approved, he will receive the crown of life which the Lord has promised to those who love Him.

2. **What two levels of economic status does James address? What does economic status have to do with trials?**

3. **Mark the references to nature. How does he use them as metaphors for those in a position of wealth?**

4. **Circle the key words from verse twelve and define them in your own words.**

Memory Verse

"But the brother of humble circumstances is to glory in his high position; and the rich man is to glory in his humiliation, because like flowering grass he will pass away."

James 1:9-10

PREPARE YOUR HEART {♥}

5. What result of genuine faith is identified in this passage?

6. What are your initial thoughts about these truths?

7. Be still before the Lord. Ask the Holy Spirit to teach, mature, and guide you this week.

Day Two
Rich Man, Poor Man

> Read James 1:9-12

James encourages the believer to see eternal advantages, no matter his social or economic position. Just as the brother "of humble circumstances" often signifies low status and powerlessness in society, so "the rich man" often has the sense of high position and power in society.

8. Read 1 Peter 1:3-4. How are both rich and poor equals by faith in Christ? What is each to glory in, according to James? Explain.

9. How can the conditions of poverty constitute a trial? How can they constitute opportunities to mature and rejoice? (cf. 1 Corinthians 1:26-31 for further insight)

10. How can the conditions of wealth constitute a trial? How can they constitute opportunities to mature and rejoice? (cf. 1 Timothy 6:6-10, 17 for further insight)

"As the poor brother forgets all his earthly poverty, so the rich brother forgets all his earthly riches. By faith in Christ the two are equals."[1]

Key Terms

Rich (*plousios*): "one who has fullness of goods."

Humble circumstances (*tapeinos*): lowly, mean, insignificant, weak, poor; one who is financially poor.

11. Why do you think James spends more time addressing the state of the rich over that of the poor?

Grass and wildflowers in the Palestinian region are abundant in the spring. They pass away quickly, however, with the beginning of the hot and dry summer season. Just as with rapidly fading flowers, life is transitory. Though the poor will also die, they never really "bloom" like the rich.

12. Read the following verses and record what you discover regarding the transitory nature of wealth.

Proverbs 18:11

Jeremiah 9:23-24

Matthew 6:19

1 Timothy 6:7

It is not particularly spiritual to be poor any more than it is particularly sinful to be rich. Read this wise prayer from Proverbs.

Keep deception and lies far from me,
Give me neither poverty nor riches;
Feed me with the food that is my portion,
That I not be full and deny You and say, "Who is the Lord?"
Or that I not be in want and steal,
And profane the name of my God.

Proverbs 30:8-9

13. Trials and temptations exist both for the rich and the poor. Consider your own attitude regarding your personal economic status. Ask God to help you improve your attitude and subsequent actions as you seek to trust and honor Him with the handling of your finances.

Notes

Notes

DIGGING DEEPER

Solomon was the tenth son of David, the second of Bathsheba, and the third king of Israel. He reigned for forty years and was chosen by God to build the temple. Even though he was very wise, he was not always very smart. We read in the Old Testament that in spite of his great wisdom, riches, status, privilege, and splendor, he fell victim to greed, pride, success, luxury, lust, and idolatry. He began his reign from a position of allegiance to God (1 Kings 8:23, 58).

Using the verses listed, summarize Solomon's spiritual and moral decline due to compromises and bad choices (1 Kings 3:1; 10:26; 11:1-6).

Solomon's book of Ecclesiastes is a collection of his reflections on life and theology. Summarize his eventual evaluation of life, and God's purposes, suggested in the following verses: Ecclesiastes 1:14, 17; 2:11, 17, 24-26; 3:1-15; 11:8.

What was his solid conclusion on the purpose of life (12:13)?

Day Three
Habakkuk's Faith

Read James 1:9-12

Habakkuk was the eighth of the Minor Prophets. His parentage and birthplace are undocumented. We know that he was a prophet of Judah, was of the tribe of Levi, was a contemporary of Jeremiah and was one of the temple singers (Habakkuk 3:19). Rabbinical tradition teaches that he was the son of the Shunammite woman whom Elisha restored to life (2 Kings 4:34-36).

14. Habakkuk was known as "the questioning prophet," always asking God "WHY?" or "HOW?" What might his boldness in approaching God indicate about his relationship with God?

"Questions and lament are part of a believer's burden, and honest dialogue with God is a necessary form of relationship with Him."[2]

Habakkuk was the one commissioned by God to take the message to unfaithful Judah that they would be punished by being delivered into Babylonian hands. At the time, Habakkuk's hopes for justice and righteousness had been raised and crushed again and again.

15. Read, and then write out rephrased and shortened summaries of Habakkuk's questions and God's answers. All verses are from the book of Habakkuk.

Habakkuk's first question (1:1-4):

God's first answser (1:5-11):

Habakkuk's second question (1:12-17):

God's second answer (2:2-20):

16. Habakkuk knew his God! What attributes of God does he mention as he asks his second question (1:12)?

What attributes of God are most meaningful to you when you are experiencing hard times?

Habakkuk's faith is strengthened by God's answers, and he voices his confidence and trust in God, evident in chapter three. The context is enduring faith in difficult times.

17. How does Habakkuk's admission of fear and frailty (3:16) help you to renew and maintain hope in the face of difficult circumstances? Note Habakkuk's review of God's past mighty acts and creative power (3:2-15).

4-6

Habakkuk's powerful confession of faith, even if reduced to total poverty, is noted in the NIV Study Bible footnote as "one of the strongest affirmations of faith in all Scripture" (3:17-18).

18. **Rewrite Habakkuk 3:17-18 in your own words to reflect your current circumstances, faith, and intentions.**

19. **Read Habakkuk 3:19. What aspect of faith does this metaphor suggest to you? How can you utilize this aspect of faith this week?**

Day Four
God's Reward for Perseverance

> Read James 1:9-12

20. **Rewrite verse twelve in your own words. Reflect on all this verse encompasses. Select one aspect meaningful to you to share with the group.**

21. **Summarize the conditions that result in a believer being blessed.**

Key Term

Blessed: The Greek term *makarios* means much more than just happy. It denotes an inner quality of life, a joy and happiness not dependent upon favorable external circumstances.

22. Match the following verses to the description of the one who is blessed.

    a) Psalm 1:1   one who trusts in the Lord

    b) Psalm 32:1-2   one who listens to wisdom (God)

    c) Psalm 34:8   one who exhibits good behavior; keeps good company

    d) Proverbs 8:34   one who obeys and honors God

    e) Isaiah 56:1-2   one who has been forgiven

    f) Jeremiah 17:7   one who takes refuge in God

23. Share some blessings you are now experiencing as a result of a personal trial victoriously and steadfastly endured.

24. Who will receive the crown of life? What assurance does this give you concerning the ultimate effect of trials you have bravely endured?

Day Five

STEPPING UP TO MATURITY

Read James 1:9-12

25. Find another place in Scripture where you can gain additional insight into victorious perseverance. What did you learn in this passage? Be prepared to share with your group.

Notes

26. Review what you have learned about *being steadfast in trials* this week. Write a principle for living a life of faith based on the passage.

27. What step(s) will you take this week to be a *doer of the Word and not a hearer only* (James 1:22)?

Notes

Lesson Five

Do Not Blame God

James 1:13-16

"Wow, a huge sale at The Shoe Cabana!" Stacy thought she had hit it big! Buying things gave her such a rush. Life had been so hard lately, but the act of purchasing something, anything, made her feel so good. Getting the bags past Mike had been proving to be harder and harder. Maybe she would leave them in the trunk this time until she had a little time to herself.

It had been a particularly hard day at work. Business had been so bad, and the threat of job loss had become a daily topic of discussion in her office. With Mike having already been laid off, shopping was really the last thing she should be doing, but the sign in the window was calling her. She justified it by knowing she would actually be saving money, and she also was getting so tired of wearing the same boring shoes. There were so many new, exciting styles, and she was missing out on them. A new pair of shoes was just what the doctor ordered!

Stacy only had to circle the block three times to find a parking spot. She thought to herself, "I'll only buy one pair." What fun it was to find the perfect pair of adorable flats to go with an outfit she bought a couple of days ago. They were a little more than she wanted to pay, but with 20% off, how could she resist? She almost made it to the checkout counter when she spotted the most amazing black suede and leather ankle boots. These would be a real splurge, but she had never seen any shoes she liked more. She resolved to not buy one more thing for a month! Besides, she really deserved something for herself to help lift her spirits.

At checkout, Stacy handed the clerk her credit card. She knew it was close to being at its credit limit, but she thought she could squeak this purchase through. She had gotten another credit card application in the mail yesterday that offered a cash advance. She had the thought that perhaps that was God's way of taking care of them in this difficult time. She could get the cash advance to help pay her bills, so this purchase really wouldn't matter all that much.

Still, during the ride home she was riddled with guilt. How could she have spent so much money when they were in over their heads already? Stacy vowed not to do it again, but thought it would be best to keep the bag in the trunk until tomorrow.

How often do you find yourself saying, "I really shouldn't, but..." Do you justify your actions or bring God into the equation? After all, He allowed the circumstances. This scenario may not be what tempts you, but every person has one or more things that do. This next section from the book of James will teach us the seriousness of giving in to temptation.

Day One
What Do I See?

1. One common temptation is some of the food we eat. What food are you most tempted by? Is it something you need to resist or can you have it any time you like?

> Read James 1:13-16

James 1:13-16

¹³Let no one say when he is tempted, "I am being tempted by God"; for God cannot be tempted by evil, and He Himself does not tempt anyone.
¹⁴But each one is tempted when he is carried away and enticed by his own lust.
¹⁵Then when lust has conceived, it gives birth to sin; and when sin is accomplished, it brings forth death.
¹⁶Do not be deceived, my beloved brethren.

2. Circle the key words of this passage. How does each word relate to these verses?

3. In light of those key words, what is the main theme of these verses?

4. What did you learn about God from this passage?

5. How is the progression of sin giving into temptation described?

Memory Verse

"Let no one say when he is tempted, 'I am being tempted by God'; for God cannot be tempted by evil, and He Himself does not tempt anyone. But each one is tempted when he is carried away and enticed by his own lust."

James 1:13-14

PREPARE YOUR HEART {♥}

6. Remembering that faith "does not blame God," what result of genuine faith is identified in this passage?

7. What are your initial thoughts about these truths?

8. Be still before the Lord. Ask the Holy Spirit to teach, mature, and guide you this week.

Day Two
Temptations vs. Trials

> Read James 1:13-16

9. Why would James bring up temptations after teaching about the trials allowed by God in the previous verses?

   What is the difference between trials and temptations?

10. Read James 1:2-4, 12-15. List the characteristics of trials and the characteristics of temptations, including any comparisons and/or contrasts you see.

Trials	Tempations

Notes

11. Why would a person blame God when encountering or succumbing to temptation?

In James 1:15, the word "death" means "separation" in the original Greek. Romans 6:23 states that "the wages of sin is death," meaning there will be an eternal separation from God for the unbeliever. However, we know that James is writing to believers. In this verse, James is not speaking of loss of salvation or eternal separation from God for believers.

12. Since James is not speaking of eternal separation from God, what do you think James means when he says, "and when sin is accomplished, it brings forth death (separation)"?

13. What is your reaction when you give into temptation? Why would it be important to you to realize the seriousness of your actions?

Can you remember a time that you downplayed the sin?

Day Three
Lessons from Scripture

Read James 1:13-16

DAVID'S BATTLE WITH TEMPTATION

14. Read 2 Samuel 11-12. According to verse 1, King David should have been out at battle, but was instead lounging around the palace. Why is this significant?

15. List the steps that describe David's progression toward sin.

16. What steps could David have taken to prevent this sin?

17. How was David restored to a right relationship with God in 2 Samuel 12?

18. What were the consequences of David's sin? What happened to those consequences after David's relationship with God was restored?

19. What principles can you glean from this passage of Scripture to apply to your own life?

DIGGING DEEPER

Our old nature seeks control of our mind. From the list of verses below (or use a concordance to find a verse you have found helpful but haven't memorized), choose one or more verse(s) to memorize. Personalize the verse if you desire (i.e. instead of "for it is God who is at work in you," try "for it is God who is at work in me"). Use this verse in times of temptation to strengthen your new self.

Romans 8:13
Galatians 5:16
Philippians 2:13
Colossians 3:5
James 4:7
1 Peter 2:11

If memorization is difficult for you, write the verse several times to help you remember it. Another idea would be to make up a melody to turn the verse into a song.

Notes

Day Four
Stopping Sin's Gestation

> Read James 1:13-16

James uses the analogy of the process of fertilization, leading to birth. In order for conception to take place, a mature, receptive egg must be available to be fertilized. That egg represents our old nature. Let's examine how we can render that egg useless and unreceptive to the temptation of sin.

20. According to James 1:14-15, at what point does temptation become sin?

21. Describe how a person can be "carried away" and "enticed" by his own lust or desire.

22. Read Mark 14:38. The command in this verse is written in a tense that indicates it is a continual action. How would the temptation to be "carried away" and "enticed" look to someone who is committed to obeying this command?

23. Record what the following verses say about using God's resources in our battle against temptation:

    Proverbs 30:5

    Romans 13:14

    Galatians 5:16-17

    Ephesians 4:22-24

    2 Peter 1:3-4

Notes

24. The Scripture gives us steps to saying "no" to temptation. Match each of the following instructions with its reference.

    ___ Value and dwell on God's Word
    ___ Realize I am no longer bound by sin
    ___ Look for the way of escape God has provided
    ___ Run the other way

    a. 1 Corinthians 10:13
    b. 1 Corinthians 10:14; 2 Timothy 2:22
    c. Romans 6:12-14; Galatians 2:20
    d. Psalm 119:9-11

25. At this point in our study of these passages, can you identify what tempts you the most? Self-control is an attribute of the Holy Spirit. Take the time now to write a prayer, offering your feelings and your mind up to God, to be controlled by Him.

Day Five
STEPPING UP TO MATURITY

Read James 1:13-16

26. Find an example in Scripture of a person who did not succumb to temptation. How did their actions affect others? What did their life reveal about their faith in God? What can you learn from their example?

27. Consider whether you ever flirt with temptation. Do you find yourself having twinges of guilt, perhaps justifying an unhealthy behavior over and over, refusing to even recognize it as sin?

28. Review what you have learned about *temptation* this week. Write a principle for living a life of faith based on this passage.

29. What step(s) will you take this week to be a *doer of the Word and not a hearer only* (James 1:22)?

Notes

Lesson Six

Respond Correctly to God's Perfect Gifts

James 1:17-18

Joey lived in a close-knit neighborhood in Portland, Oregon. He had just turned ten the winter of 1933. Times were very difficult. His father had worked for a shipbuilding company, but now he was without work. Money was so tight there was barely enough for food.

On Joey's birthday that year he knew there would be no presents. However, that morning a package appeared on the front porch with Joey's name on it. Joey's face beamed! Had Mom and Dad found some way to get him a gift? No, Mom and Dad were just as surprised as Joey. Joey opened the package, and inside was a brand new pair of shoes in his exact size. Oh, how he needed shoes! He had been stuffing cardboard in the soles to keep the cold and water from coming through.

The very next morning there was another present with his name on it. What could be in this box? Joey tore the package open to find a new coat, also in his exact size. No more newspaper insulation in his old worn-out coat!

Joey never forgot that winter, for there were more packages that arrived, always anonymously. There were packages of pants, shirts, hats, mittens, and chocolate bars. Joey found out that every child in his school was receiving things in the same way; however, none of the families ever figured out where the gifts were coming from.

The children's teacher never told them that her uncle was the owner of the shipbuilding company that had had to lay off the fathers of these children during the depression. He had asked her to find out the sizes and the needs of each child in that one-room school. He then set out to provide for each exact need.

Joey and the children grew into adults, but never forgot the gifts they received that winter. In fact, as an adult Joey made it a point to look for opportunities to give to those in need.

The passage we are about to study in James reveals the nature of God, who gives us new life and exactly what we need to perfect us in our faith. In response to His perfect gifts, we are to offer our lives back to Him.

Day One
What Do I See?

1. Do you know of someone who is good at giving gifts? What do you think makes them good at gift giving? What qualities make something a good gift?

> Read James 1:17-18

James 1:17-18

¹⁷Every good thing given and every perfect gift is from above, coming down from the Father of lights, with whom there is no variation or shifting shadow. ¹⁸In the exercise of His will He brought us forth by the word of truth, so that we would be a kind of first fruits among His creatures.

2. List everything this passage tells you about the nature of God.

3. What do these verses tell you about the characteristics of God's gifts?

4. What do you think would make a "perfect" gift from God's perspective (Hint: See James 1:2-4)?

5. Rewrite James 1:18, personalizing how and why you were brought forth by God.

PREPARE YOUR HEART {♥}

6. What result of genuine faith is identified in this passage?

7. What are your initial thoughts about these truths?

8. Be still before the Lord. Ask the Holy Spirit to teach, mature, and guide you this week.

Memory Verse

"Every good thing given and every perfect gift is from above, coming down from the Father of lights, with whom there is no variation or shifting shadow."

James 1:17

Day Two
God's Gifts Are Always Good

> Read James 1:17-18

9. In James 1:17, the Greek word for "perfect" means complete, mature, fully developed, finished. In light of that definition, what would that say about gifts from God?

PAUL'S FAITH

In the beginning of 2 Corinthians 12, Paul speaks of his personal experience of being caught up to heaven and hearing inexpressible words while there.

10. Read 2 Corinthians 12:7-10. From 2 Corinthians 12:7, Paul describes that he had been in danger of being tempted by what sin?

11. What did God allow in Paul's life that helped him with that temptation?

12. How do we know that Paul did not immediately embrace this?

13. To learn from Paul's example, what should a believer first do when faced with a difficult situation? How does this relate with James 1:5 from our previous study?

14. Read Romans 8:28. How did God use this situation in Paul's life?

15. Can you think of something that happened in the past that you had trouble accepting, but God used it for your good?

The Greek word for "perfect" means complete, mature, fully developed, finished.

Day Three

Perfect Gifts Come from an Unchanging God

Read James 1:17-18

16. God is described as "the Father of lights" in verse 17. What does this mean (see also Psalm 136:7-9)?

17. What is the difference between the nature of the Creator and the nature of His creation as described in the last part of verse 17?

18. Record what the following verses say about the unchanging nature of God:

    Numbers 23:19

    Psalm 102:25-27

    Malachi 3:6

    Hebrews 13:8

19. Why is it important to know that you have an unchanging God when trials and temptations come into your life?

20. God cannot get more perfect. God's plan for our lives cannot be improved upon. Thank God for His unchanging nature and the plan He has in place for the perfecting of your faith.

Day Four

A Great Gift with a Great Purpose

> Read James 1:17-18

21. What is the significance of us being brought forth by "the exercise of His will"?

22. Read 2 Timothy 1:8-9. What other details about our calling can be found in these verses?

23. The method God used in bringing us forth to salvation was the gospel. God's Word proclaims the message of the work of Jesus Christ, and the power of the Holy Spirit brings new life to the hearts of those who hear and receive the truth of that message. Record what the following verses say about God's Word:

    Romans 1:16

    Romans 10:17

    1 Thessalonians 2:13

    1 Peter 1:23

"First fruits" is an Old Testament term that the Jewish believers James is speaking to would be familiar with. Israel had been instructed by God that the first portion of a harvest or the firstborn animal belonged to God. It was to be presented to God as His possession, and was considered holy.

24. As God's first fruits, brought forth from death to life through an act of God's will, ask God for wisdom as to how He wants to use you. What would change in your life if you offered yourself back to God, holy and to be used for His purpose?

DIGGING DEEPER

Use your computer to go to www.blueletterbible.org/search. Use the Bible Search to look up "first fruits" in this concordance tool. We would recommend changing the Bible version tab to NASB (New American Standard Bible).

Record what further aspects of the term "first fruits" you see as you read through the verses displayed on your computer screen.

Day Five

STEPPING UP TO MATURITY

Read James 1:17-18

25. Find an example in Scripture of a person who received God's great gift of salvation and then offered themselves completely back to Him. What did their life reveal about their faith in God? What can you learn from this example?

26. Review what you have learned about *God's perfect gifts* this week. Write a principle for living a life of faith based on this passage.

27. What step(s) will you take this week to be a *doer of the Word and not a hearer only* (James 1:22)?

Lesson Seven

Respond Correctly to God's Word

James 1:19-27

Joan and Nancy had worked together in the same office for almost five years, and both women attended the same church. Last Sunday's message at church had dealt with the topic of the works of the old nature. One of the things their pastor talked about Sunday was gossiping. Both Joan and Nancy struggled with office politics, and they often talked with their co-workers about other people in their department.

Sitting in the break room on Monday morning, Joan confessed to Nancy that Sunday's sermon had spoken to her in a mighty way. Joan told Nancy that she had asked several women to pray for her and hold her accountable during the week. Nancy smiled politely and said, "Good for you, Joan." But Nancy had had a lot on her mind Sunday, and she really didn't remember the sermon. In fact, Nancy remembered telling her husband that she had found the sermon boring.

The week seemed to go quickly. Joan spent time every morning in God's Word. She asked God daily for the strength and wisdom to control her tongue. She got several calls from women checking in with her. Joan made it through the week by quietly excusing herself from groups when gossip started. When Friday came, Joan was unexpectedly cornered at the copier by a co-worker named Cassie, who had some juicy news. Joan had to finish her task, so she couldn't excuse herself. What would she do?

Her mind flashed back to Sunday's message and the Scripture she had just read that morning. Joan said a quick prayer, and she was filled with peace. She gently told her co-worker that she was uncomfortable talking about others, and asked if they could change the subject. The coworker was surprised at Joan's response, but graciously agreed to end the gossip.

A couple of hours later, Nancy saw Joan and excitedly rushed over. Unfortunately, the first words out of Nancy's mouth were, "I've got to tell you what Cassie just told me!"

This story illustrates the truth from James we are studying this week. Both women had been exposed to the same truth from God's Word, but only one had made it a priority to study it intently. This allowed the light of God's Word to expose her sin, and God's Word also provided the way to gain victory over it.

Day One
What Do I See?

1. Think of a time you did not listen to and/or follow instructions, and then later wished you had. Describe the situation and the result.

> **Read James 1:19-27**

James 1:19-27

¹⁹This you know, my beloved brethren. But everyone must be quick to hear, slow to speak and slow to anger;
²⁰for the anger of man does not achieve the righteousness of God.
²¹Therefore, putting aside all filthiness and all that remains of wickedness, in humility receive the word implanted, which is able to save your souls.
²²But prove yourselves doers of the word, and not merely hearers who delude themselves.
²³For if anyone is a hearer of the word and not a doer, he is like a man who looks at his natural face in a mirror;
²⁴for once he has looked at himself and gone away, he has immediately forgotten what kind of person he was.
²⁵But one who looks intently at the perfect law, the law of liberty, and abides by it, not having become a forgetful hearer but an effectual doer, this man will be blessed in what he does.
²⁶If anyone thinks himself to be religious, and yet does not bridle his tongue but deceives his own heart, this man's religion is worthless.
²⁷Pure and undefiled religion in the sight of our God and Father is this: to visit orphans and widows in their distress, and to keep oneself unstained by the world.

2. Circle the key words or phrases repeated in these verses.

3. Based on those key words, what do you think is the major theme of this text?

4. What is the illustration used to contrast the "hearer" and the "doer" of the Word?

5. In James 1:26-27, underline the outward signs of true religion.

Memory Verse

"But prove yourselves doers of the word, and not merely hearers who delude themselves."

James 1:22

PREPARE YOUR HEART

6. What result of genuine faith is identified in this passage?

7. What are your initial thoughts about this passage?

8. Be still before the Lord. Ask the Holy Spirit to teach, mature, and guide you this week.

Day Two
How to Receive God's Word

Read James 1:19-27

At the beginning of James 1:19, the words "this you know" are referring specifically to the transforming power of God's Word (described in James 1:18). We know this ... that we have been brought forth by the Word of Truth.

9. **In the chart below, list the consequences that could be associated with not obeying the instructions found in James 1:19, along with practical ways you can obey each command.**

RESPONSE TO GOD'S WORD	CONSEQUENCES OF NOT OBEYING	PRACTICAL WAYS TO OBEY
Quick to Hear		
Slow to Speak		
Slow to Anger		

10. What do these commands reveal about the attitude a believer should have toward God's Word?

11. In order for God's Word to perform its work in a believer's life, what is the believer's responsibility according to James 1:21?

"Where there is life there will be growth. Practical faith in the Word should naturally grow into practical obedience to the Word. That same 'Word of Truth' that produces life is able to nourish and sustain life. Faith and obedience go hand in hand."[1]

12. Record each passage's explanation about how we need to change our relationship with sin.

   Ephesians 4:22-24

   Colossians 3:5-10

   Hebrews 12:1-2

   1 Peter 2:1

When James says the implanted word "is able to save your souls," he is not speaking of salvation. The Word implanted in a believer's life provides continual power to fight the battle that has been waged against our souls by the world, the flesh, and the devil. Believers cannot lose their salvation, but can lose their effectiveness for God.

13. What do you think it means to receive God's Word with meekness or humility?

14. Ask for God's wisdom as you examine your "soul." Try to identify any sin that you have allowed to remain in your heart. Perhaps it is something that you have permitted, thinking that it won't really matter. Take the time now to confess your sin and to ask God for help to overcome this sin in the future.

Day Three

Mirror, Mirror on the Wall

Read James 1:19-27

15. Verse 21 tells us that God implants His Word in us. Describe how a farmer or gardener makes certain a seed grows to be mature and healthy.

16. Read 2 Timothy 3:16-17. If we carefully cultivate the Word of God in our heart, what can we expect as a result?

The Word implanted in a believer's life provides continual power to fight the battle that has been waged against our souls by the world, the flesh and the devil.

17. Read James 1:22-25. In the chart below, list the characteristics of the one who is a doer of the Word, and the characteristics of the one who is only a hearer of the Word.

HEARERS ONLY	HEARERS AND DOERS

18. Why do you think James used a mirror as an illustration of God's Word?

19. Read Hebrews 4:12. What does this verse say about the revealing power of God's Word?

James 1:25 tells us the "doer" will be blessed in what he does. This is a blessing we receive from God, but it is not a reward He gives *after* we do a work for Him. The blessing we receive comes in the actual performance of the work. We are blessed *in* the doing.

20. Try to remember a time when you were doing a work for the Lord and you received a great blessing from doing that work. Share the details.

Notes

Day Four
Outward Proof of an Inward Change

> Read James 1:19-27

Our faith is tested by the response we have to the Word of God. Being obedient to God's Word is not a list of do's and don'ts, mixed with religious-looking habits. God's Word provides the power to change our hearts and priorities, and then the Word will guide us to be obedient to do God's will.

21. James 1:26 tells us that the person who does not bridle his tongue deceives his heart. Read the following verses and record what they say about the relationship between the mouth and the heart.

    Psalm 37:30-31

    Matthew 15:18

    Luke 6:45

    Romans 10:9-10

22. How long has it been since you reached out to encourage a brother or sister in need? Who is God bringing to mind that you can reach out to now?

SAMUEL'S FAITH

23. Read 1 Samuel 1:19-28 and 2:11-21. What circumstances brought Samuel to Shiloh?

24. Samuel was left in the care of Eli at the temple of the Lord. According to these verses in 1 Samuel, what other influences would Samuel be exposed to at the temple?

25. Read 1 Samuel 3. The Word of the Lord came to Samuel. How do we know that he was not influenced by the sinful actions of Eli's sons as he grew older?

26. Although God's Word came to Samuel audibly, His written Word to us is just as personal and life-changing. What does this account teach you?

27. How does this apply to your life today?

DIGGING DEEPER

Read 1 Samuel 2:1-10. This is Hannah's song to God when she brought Samuel to give him to the service of the Lord. Read this prayer and then describe what Hannah's prayer reveals about her convictions and her knowledge of God. How do you think this knowledge helped her when she had to leave her son with Eli? How would the knowledge of God through His Word help you when you are called to do a seemingly impossible task?

Day Five

STEPPING UP TO MATURITY

Read James 1:19-27

28. Find an example in Scripture of a person who heard the Word of the Lord and did not respond by becoming a "doer." How did their actions affect others? What did their life reveal about their faith in God? What could they have done differently to follow what James is teaching in this passage? What can you learn from their example?

29. Review what you learned about *responding properly to God's Word* this week. Write a principle for living a life of faith based on this passage.

30. What step(s) will you take this week to be a *doer of the Word and not a hearer only* (James 1:22)?

Notes

Lesson Eight

Do Not Show Favoritism, Part 1

James 2:1-7

She lived two doors down in the same dorm as Evie. Cathy walked by Evie's room several times a day, often times seeing her but never making eye contact. She felt bad once in a while when she had gone out of her way to avoid her, but she rationalized Evie wasn't her type. Cathy made it a point to dress nicely and to never go out without running a hair brush through her hair. Evie, on the other hand, was always sweaty, unkempt, and rough around the edges. Cathy stuck close to her friends, welcoming only those that were like her. Evie just didn't fit the mold.

Two days before graduation, rushing from one final exam to the other, Cathy ran straight into Evie; four years of sharing just a "hi" in the hall culminated in an awkward exchange. Later that day Evie knocked on her door to return the book that Cathy had dropped. For the first time Cathy took a moment to look past the hard exterior, and saw in Evie's dark eyes a kindness and genuine thoughtfulness that she had never bothered to see before.

As Evie turned to leave with a quick "good-bye," Cathy watched her disappear into her room down the hall. Cathy realized they could have been friends, but now it was too late. They were about ready to graduate and go their separate ways. Cathy had missed an opportunity with Evie that she would never get back.

James speaks of favoritism that doesn't just take place in a dorm, but in the church where pews aren't shared and lives refuse to be intertwined. James encourages us that faith will break down those barriers!

Day One
What Do I See?

1. When has someone helped you to feel welcomed in a new or uncomfortable situation?

> **Read James 2:1-13**

James 2:1-7

¹My brethren, do not hold your faith in our glorious Lord Jesus Christ with an attitude of personal favoritism.
²For if a man comes into your assembly with a gold ring and dressed in fine clothes, and there also comes in a poor man in dirty clothes,
³and you pay special attention to the one who is wearing the fine clothes, and say, "You sit here in a good place," and you say to the poor man, "You stand over there, or sit down by my footstool,"
⁴have you not made distinctions among yourselves, and become judges with evil motives?
⁵Listen, my beloved brethren: did not God choose the poor of this world to be rich in faith and heirs of the kingdom which He promised to those who love Him?
⁶But you have dishonored the poor man. Is it not the rich who oppress you and personally drag you into court?
⁷Do they not blaspheme the fair name by which you have been called?

2. Circle the key words of this passage. Using a Bible Dictionary, concordance or www.biblegateway.com, look up the meaning of each key word and write your own definition.

3. Underline the contrasts in the passage above.

4. Where is this situation taking place? Why is the location significant?

Memory Verse

"My brethren, do not hold your faith in our glorious Lord Jesus Christ with an attitude of personal favoritism."

James 2:1

5. List the key characters in this passage.

6. What command does James give?

PREPARE YOUR HEART {♥}

7. What result of genuine faith is identified in this passage?

8. What are your initial thoughts about these truths?

9. Be still before the Lord. Ask the Holy Spirit to teach, mature, and guide you this week.

Day Two
Needed: A New Point of View

> Read James 2:1-7

10. In the chart below, record how the two men were treated:

RICH MAN	POOR MAN

11. What determined the treatment of visitors to the church?

Notes

12. This was not a new problem; consider 1 Samuel 16:7. Note the contrast between God's and man's perspective.

13. What did the favoritism shown by the church members reveal about their heart condition (verse 4)?

Without a heart change their actions would never change.

James's strong reprimand was important for the believers to hear. Without a heart change, their actions would never change. The same is true for believers today. Take some time to evaluate your own motives behind the way you treat others. Ask God to cleanse your heart from evil motives (Psalm 51:10).

14. In what ways does God view the poor (verse 5)?

    What additional insight does James 1:9-11 provide?

15. Record how God treated the poor and needy in the following passages:

    Deuteronomy 7:7-8

    Deuteronomy 10:17-18

    Psalm 68:10

    Psalm 113:5-9

    What does God's treatment of the poor and needy reveal about how He views them?

16. What did the believers' treatment of the poor and needy reveal about how they viewed the poor (verse 6)?

   What does your treatment of the poor and needy reveal about your view of the poor?

17. What does James point out about the behavior of the rich (verses 6-7)?

   How does the rich man's behavior point out the foolishness of the believers' treatment of the poor?

   In what ways do you see this kind of treatment carried out in the church today?

Day Three
Jesus' Life of Faith

> Read James 2:1-7

18. There will be no distinctions in heaven, no second class citizens. What did God promise to ALL who loved Him?

   In what ways do the blessings and benefits of eternity discourage believers from showing partiality today?

   If you viewed others with eternity in mind, how would your perception of them change?

Notes

DIGGING DEEPER

Using a Bible Dictionary or commentary, research what is included in being "rich in faith and heirs of the kingdom," from James 2:5.

Consider Jesus' example. Jesus, God incarnate, the glorious Lord, showed no favoritism. It made no difference to Jesus whether the one He was speaking to was a wealthy Jewish leader or a lowly prostitute. He loved and cared for each person with whom He came in contact.

19. In the chart below, record the person, their position, and Jesus' response to that individual:

SCRIPTURE	THE PERSON AND THEIR POSITION	JESUS' RESPONSE TO THEM
Matthew 9:18-26		
Luke 17:11-14		
Luke 19:2, 5, 8		
John 4:7-14		

What characteristics were consistent in Jesus' interaction with people of varying backgrounds?

How does Jesus' example encourage you to interact with people you come into contact with during a typical day? Consider specific people.

Day Four
Following Jesus' Example

Read James 2:1-7

Setting the ultimate example, "...God demonstrates His own love toward us, in that while we were yet sinners, Christ died for us" (Romans 5:8). Despite our sin-filled lives and worthlessness, Jesus honored us by dying for each of us.

20. In what ways does Jesus' willingness to die for you affect the way you think of and treat others?

21. God gives us directions for following Jesus' example. Match each of the following instructions with its reference:

    Humility _____
    Looking out for others _____
    Through love, serve one another _____
    Be subject to one another _____
    Accept one another _____

    a. Romans 15:7
    b. Galatians 5:13
    c. Ephesians 5:21
    d. Philippians 2:3
    e. Philippians 2:4

    Consider each attribute above. For each, consider ways you can demonstrate this quality in your life.

    Humility

    Looking out for others

    Through love, serve one another

    Be subject to one another

    Accept one another

Notes

22. What has the potential to be different in your life, in your church, or in your area of ministry if you follow these instructions?

Day Five
STEPPING UP TO MATURITY

> Read James 2:1-7

23. Who in Scripture is an example of someone who did not show favoritism? How did their actions affect others? What did their life reveal about their faith in God? What can you learn from their example?

24. Consider your own responses and interactions with various people. Who are you most likely to show favoritism to? Why? Refer to the list at the side to get you started. Evaluate the motives behind your actions.

25. Review what you have discovered about *showing favoritism* this week. Write a principle for living a life of faith based on this passage.

26. What step(s) will you take this week to be a *doer of the Word, and not a hearer only* (James 1:22)?

Areas to Consider
Poorly dressed
Physically handicapped
Mentally disabled
Needy
Different socio-economic status
Racial differences
Different education status
Parenting style
Working class
The influential

Lesson Nine

Do Not Show Favoritism, Part 2

James 2:8-13

You would have thought it was her first time at church the way she slipped in and out unnoticed, but it wasn't. Of course, the woman sitting a few seats over did shake her hand during the "meet and greet" that occurred every Sunday between the first and second song. Other than that, it was as though Maria was invisible.

She even tried showing up at special women's events, hoping to find a friend, at least a friendly smile. It seemed, however, that everyone already had a "buddy." She often left feeling lonelier than when she arrived. Maria knew she wasn't quite like them; she came from the other side of town, her husband had left her long ago, and she couldn't afford the cute styles the other women wore. Maria's dreams of finding a place where she could be a part of a family and be loved and accepted were fading fast. But hadn't Jesus reached out to the poor and lonely? Weren't His people supposed to do the same? What was faith supposed to look like anyway?

James left believers a clear description so that there wouldn't be any invisible, lonely Marias in our church pews.

Day One

What Do I See?

1. When have you experienced positive or negative "favoritism"? How did it make you feel?

> **Read James 2:1-13**

James 2:8-13

⁸If, however, you are fulfilling the royal law according to the Scripture, "YOU SHALL LOVE YOUR NEIGHBOR AS YOURSELF," you are doing well.
⁹But if you show partiality, you are committing sin and are convicted by the law as transgressors.
¹⁰For whoever keeps the whole law and yet stumbles in one point, he has become guilty of all.
¹¹For He who said, "DO NOT COMMIT ADULTERY," also said, "DO NOT COMMIT MURDER." Now if you do not commit adultery, but do commit murder, you have become a transgressor of the law.
¹²So speak and so act as those who are to be judged by the law of liberty.
¹³For judgment will be merciless to one who has shown no mercy; mercy triumphs over judgment.

2. Circle the key words in this passage.

3. Underline the commands.

4. What contrast is being made?

PREPARE YOUR HEART {♥}

5. What result of genuine fatih is identified in this passage?

6. How have your initial thoughts about this truth changed since last week?

7. Be still before the Lord. Ask the Holy Spirit to teach, mature, and guide you this week.

Memory Verse

"If, however, you are fulfilling the royal law according to the Scripture, ·YOU SHALL LOVE YOUR NEIGHBOR AS YOURSELF,· you are doing well."

James 2:8

Day Two
Keeping the Royal Law: Loving My Neighbor

> Read James 2:8-13

8. How does James define the Royal Law?

9. What practical ways do you care for your own spiritual, physical, and emotional well being?

   In what practical ways can you demonstrate the Royal Law to others?

10. Why would James say, "If you are fulfilling the Royal Law, you are doing well" (cf. 1 John 4:7-8, 11)?

11. Evaluate your life. In what areas are you doing well? Where might you need to improve?

DIGGING DEEPER

Consider other passages that deal with how the poor are to be treated. Based on the information you gather, write a description of how all believers are to treat the poor.

Other Occurrences of the Royal Law:

Matthew 22:34-40
Romans 13:9
Galatians 5:14

Day Three

Keeping the Royal Law: Loving My Neighbor, Part 2

> Read James 2:8-13

The Greek word for love in verse 8 is *agape*. "This word, *agape*, describes a love that is based on the deliberate choice of the one who loves rather than the worthiness of the one who is loved. This kind of love goes against natural human inclination. It is a giving, selfless, expect-nothing-in-return kind of love."[1] Agape love is a choice, not an emotion, and always takes action. Jesus illustrated this kind of love in the story of the Good Samaritan.

THE EXAMPLE OF THE GOOD SAMARITAN

> Read Luke 10:25-37

12. Record the responses to the injured man in the chart:

THE CHARACTER	THE RESPONSE
The Priest	
The Levite	
The Samaritan	

13. Based on this passage, what conclusions can you draw about who God considers our neighbors to be?

Samaritans were considered half breeds as a result of the inner marrying between the Jews and the Gentiles; as a result, bitter animosity existed between the Samaritans and the Jews when the Samaritans built a rival temple on Mount Gerizim.

14. From man's perspective, and considering cultural influences, which of the three would have been considered "religious"? Why?

15. Which of the three should have treated the injured man as a neighbor? Which one actually did?

16. Read 1 Corinthians 13:4-8. Which characteristics of love were demonstrated by the Samaritan, and how did he show them?

17. Describe a time when you were treated with one of these characteristics of love. What was the result?

When have you recently demonstrated one of these characteristics of love? What was the result?

Day Four

Breaking the Law: Showing Partiality

> Read James 2:8-13

18. List the results of showing partiality (verses 9-11).

What do these results reveal about the seriousness of showing partiality?

How does this affect the way you tolerate your own demonstration of partiality to others?

19. What would look different in your life if you focused on keeping the "Royal Law"? Consider how that would affect your encounters with those you know personally and those you don't.

Day Five
STEPPING UP TO MATURITY

> Read James 2:8-13

20. In what ways might the "Law of Liberty" influence believers' interactions with others (verse 13)?

21. Look up "mercy" in a Bible Dictionary and write your own definition.

    How has God shown mercy to you?

    How does considering God's mercy in your own life motivate you to show mercy to others? Who could you purposefully show mercy to this week?

22. If one refuses to show mercy to others, what does that reveal about their faith?

Notes

23. Find an example in Scripture of a person who showed favoritism. How did their actions affect others? What did their life reveal about their faith in God? What can you learn from their example?

24. Review the principle for living a life of faith you wrote last week (#25). Considering what you have learned this week, is there anything you would change or add? Rewrite it here.

25. What step(s) will you take this week to be a *doer of the Word and not a hearer only* (James 1:22)?

Notes

Lesson Ten

Show Faith Through Works

James 2:14-20

There was a brother and a sister who were all alone in a building after a devastating earthquake. They had no idea where their parents were because they were at school when the earthquake hit. Huddled together under a sturdy table, they waited for someone to find them. The brother continually tried to calm his younger sister's fears while she cried out for her mommy. He would hum, rock her and stroke her hair as he had seen his mother do many times before. But he himself had doubting thoughts, "What if no one comes looking for us? What will we eat? Do we still have a house to live in? Where are our mom and dad?" There were too many questions for his young mind to wrap around, questions that seemed to have no answers.

Then in the distance he thought he heard a dog bark. "Must be a lost dog looking for its owner, wondering where its family is just like us." The barking seemed to be getting closer. The little boy cried out as loud as he could, "We're over here! Over here!" He really didn't know why he cried out, but the dog's bark seemed to be saying, "Where are you? I'm looking for you!" His sister started yelling also.

They continued to cry out for what seemed like an eternity. Finally, there seemed to be a slight sound coming from beside them. Then a bit of the rubble surrounding them seemed to move. "Oh no," thought the brother, "Another earthquake?" Suddenly, faint light streamed into the darkness of the area under their table. The whole area was filled with light. The dog barked louder, and they began to also hear people's voices. The boy's heart leaped in his chest, they were saved!

What happened next? Did the people look in at the brother and sister and say, "Oh there you are! Good! Now you will be fine! See you later!" No, they surely would have followed through and given the children food and water and put blankets around them, and then found them shelter right away. The rescuers would see a need, and act on it immediately; no hesitation. This is what James speaks of when he says, "In the same way, faith by itself, if it is not accompanied by action, is dead" (James 2:17, NIV).

Day One
What Do I See?

1. Recall a time when you started a project but your heart wasn't in it. How did the project turn out? Now share a time when you worked on a project in which you were interested. What became of that project?

> **Read James 2:14-20**

James 2:14-20

¹⁴What use is it, my brethren, if someone says he has faith but he has no works? Can that faith save him?

¹⁵If a brother or sister is without clothing and in need of daily food,

¹⁶and one of you says to them, "Go in peace, be warmed and be filled," and yet you do not give them what is necessary for their body, what use is that?

¹⁷Even so faith, if it has no works, is dead, being by itself.

¹⁸But someone may well say, "You have faith and I have works; show me your faith without the works, and I will show you my faith by my works."

¹⁹You believe that God is one. You do well; the demons also believe, and shudder.

²⁰But are you willing to recognize, you foolish fellow, that faith without works is useless?

2. **Circle the repeated words in this passage. Define each of these key words. Make a list of any adjectives or descriptive words you find in these definitions.**

3. What was James contrasting in verse 18?

PREPARE YOUR HEART {♥}

4. What result of genuine faith is identified in this passage?

Memory Verse

"Even so faith, if it has no works, is dead, being by itself."

James 2:17

5. What are your initial thoughts about these truths?

6. Be still before the Lord. Ask the Holy Spirit to teach, mature, and guide you this week.

Day Two

Can Words Alone Warm the Heart?

Read James 2:14-20

7. In James 2:26, we read, "...faith without works is dead." What are some other phrases James used to convey this idea in the following verses?

VERSE	PHRASE
14	
17	
18	
20	

8. A person who claims to live faithfully should show evidence. What example is given in verses 15 and 16 to illustrate this principle?

What does faith that doesn't produce works look like?

What should faith look like? Where do you see this in your life?

Notes

9. In the following verses, how should believers treat others?

    Matthew 5:37-48

    Galatians 6:10

    Hebrews 13:2

    James 1:27

    1 John 3:16-18

10. Evaluate the way you treat others. What might be hindering you from treating others as God would want?

11. How will you apply these truths to your walk this week so you will not be hindered?

Day Three
Lydia's Faith

> Read Acts 16:14-15, 40

12. What do we learn about Lydia's background from these verses?

13. After accepting Paul's message, what steps did Lydia take?

14. Where do you see evidence of her faith?

15. How do her actions encourage you in your faith?

16. Read Galatians 6:10. How does this verse encourage you?

Day Four
Knowledge vs. Faith

> Read James 2:19-20

Acknowledgement that there is a God is good, but what exactly does that acknowledgment mean? Even the demons believe in God, but they do not obey God's Word or follow Jesus' example. Many claim to know God, but their actions don't reveal obedience to Scripture or a desire to imitate Christ.

17. James references Deuteronomy 6:4. Write down this verse:

    How does this relate to the James passage?

    Why did James make this reference? What point was James trying to make? (Note: Deuteronomy 6:4 was the Shema, which which became Judaism's basic confession and affirmation of faith. It was recited morning and night.)

18. Read Deuteronomy 6:5-6. What do these verses command us to "do"?

    If someone stopped reading at verse 4, what would they be missing?

"So then, my beloved, just as you have always obeyed, not as in my presence only, but now much more in my absence, work out your salvation with fear and trembling; for it is God who is at work in you, both to will and to work for His good pleasure."

Philippians 2:12-13

19. Tell the Lord how much you love Him. Record your prayer here.

DIGGING DEEPER

James states in verse 19 that it is good to believe in the oneness of God, but so do the demons. How do we know this? Look up these Scriptures and note what the demons believed in.

Matthew 8:28-33

Mark 1:23-27

Mark 3:11-12

Day Five

STEPPING UP TO MATURITY

| Read James 2:14-20 |

20. Find an example of a person in Scripture that talked of having faith, but did not display it in their lives. How did their actions affect others? What did their life reveal about their faith in God? What can you learn from their example?

Notes

21. James wanted his fellow believers to meditate on the truths we studied this week, and then put these into practice. Take time to examine your faith this week. How has it grown through this study?

22. Review what you have discovered about *showing faith through works* this week. Write a principle for living a life of faith based on this week's passage.

23. What step(s) will you take this week to be a *doer of the Word and not a hearer only* (James 1:22)?

Notes

Lesson Eleven

Take Action

James 2:21-26

What an honor! Just a sophomore, but he had been selected to travel with the varsity baseball team. He could hardly wait to get his cleats on and play with the "big boys." Boarding a plane and heading to Arizona for a week of baseball was a young man's dream come true.

The week was filled with fun, competition, and sunshine. His hope was to impress the coach and get acquainted with the varsity boys in hopes he would be joining them the next spring. All seemed to be going well – he had actually made some challenging plays in the field, and had even gotten a couple of hits off of the faster pitching. He had joined in some harmless pranks with the guys after lights out. Brett sensed that he was fitting in just fine and that he had not only a chance at some more playing time during the trip, but that the coach was seriously considering him for a position on the team for next year.

His dad had talked to him before he left about the possibility of some "questionable activities" that he might be expected to be a part of, but so far, so good! The guys that he already knew on the team knew that Brett was a believer and that he didn't frequent the parties that many of them attended. Maybe his dad was wrong. Nothing had seemed questionable yet. At least not until the coach announced that as a special treat, he would be taking the guys out to dinner at a restaurant known for the waitresses wearing low-cut, tight shirts. By the guys' response, it was obvious they weren't going for the great burgers.

Brett had a choice to make! Sure, he believed in Jesus; he had put his faith in Christ when he was a child. He had grown up under the care of Christian parents, but this moment was an opportunity like he had never had before. He could blend in with his teammates, laugh at the coarse jokes that were sure to be flying back and forth at the dinner table, and ogle the girls as they passed by, trying not to make waves in hope of securing his spot on the team. Or he could choose to live out his faith and say "no" to putting himself in a situation that he knew would not be honoring to his Savior. Was his faith real? Did it matter outside of church on Sunday mornings and youth groups on Wednesday nights?

James, a follower of Jesus, speaks to faith that takes action. Thankfully, Brett chose to live out his faith. He walked right on by that restaurant door. As his team members walked in, he walked by! Faith, after all, without actions is dead. Brett's faith was alive and well. And his baseball skills must have spoken for themselves; he secured himself a starting position on the team for the next year.

Day One
What Do I See?

1. Have you ever gone on vacation and forgotten to care for your yard? What happened?

> Read James 2:21-26

James 2:21-26

²¹Was not Abraham our father justified by works when he offered up Isaac his son on the altar?
²²You see that faith was working with his works, and as a result of the works, faith was perfected;
²³and the Scripture was fulfilled which says, "AND ABRAHAM BELIEVED GOD, AND IT WAS RECKONED TO HIM AS RIGHTEOUSNESS," and he was called the friend of God.
²⁴You see that a man is justified by works and not by faith alone.
²⁵In the same way, was not Rahab the harlot also justified by works when she received the messengers and sent them out by another way?
²⁶For just as the body without the spirit is dead, so also faith without works is dead.

2. Circle the names of people James used as examples.

3. Underline the key words (look for repeated words). Define each key word you may not know.

4. Put a box around the comparison in verse 26.

PREPARE YOUR HEART {♥}

5. What result of genuine faith is identified in this passage?

6. What are your initial thoughts about these truths?

7. Be still before the Lord. Ask the Holy Spirit to teach, mature, and guide you this week.

Memory Verse

"For just as the body without the spirit is dead, so also faith without works is dead."

James 2:26

Day Two
Faith Perfected: Abraham's Faith

> Read James 2:21-22

8. Let's take a walk through Abraham's life and the faith he displayed. Complete the chart below:

SCRIPTURE	HOW DID ABRAHAM SHOW HIS FAITH?	HOW DID GOD RESPOND?
Genesis 15:1-6		
Genesis 22:1-18		

In Genesis 22, Abraham's faith was tested to the extreme. Charles Swindoll wrote, "God knew what Abraham would do. It was Abraham who needed to see the extent of his own faith."[1]

9. James writes in James 2:21 that Abraham's willingness to sacrifice Isaac (Genesis 22) justified Abraham's faith (Genesis 15:6). How was Abraham justified by works when he was already justified by faith? What did Abraham's actions reveal about his faith?

10. Abraham heard God's command and obeyed, even though he was put in a tough situation. Is there an area of your life in which God is asking you to show your faith by taking action?

Day Three
Friend of God

> Read James 2:23-24

11. James was referring to Genesis 15:6 when he mentioned that Scripture was fulfilled. According to this verse, why did God declare Abraham righteous?

Key Term

Perfected: To complete; accomplished; finished. Abraham's works resulted in his faith being complete.

DIGGING DEEPER

The cross reference for Genesis 15:6 is Romans 4. What truths do you learn about Abraham's faith in these verses?

Key Term

Reckoned: To enroll oneself in; counted; accredited to.

Read Genesis 18:17-33

12. In this passage there is an intimate conversation between God and Abraham. How do God's answers to Abraham's questions show that Abraham was a friend of God?

13. Because you have been justified by faith, God calls you His friend as well. How do you show God that you are His friend?

Day Four

Rahab's Faith: Acting Even When There Are Risks

14. Read Joshua 2:1-24 and 6:21-25. What phrases are used to depict Rahab's knowledge of God?

What actions from these passages demonstrate her heart of faith?

11-4

15. Read Matthew 1:1, 5 and Hebrews 11:31. What blessings were given to Rahab because of her faith? Did she get to see all of these during her lifetime?

16. How does Rahab's example encourage you to act in faith in situations you are facing today?

Day Five
STEPPING UP TO MATURITY

> Read James 2:21-26

17. Find an example of a person in Scripture who took action because of their faith. How did their actions show faith in God, and in turn, show their faith to others?

18. Review what you learned about *taking action* because of your faith this week. Write a principle for living a life of faith based on this passage.

19. What step(s) will you take this week to be a *doer of the Word and not a hearer only* (James 1:22)?

"Greater love has no one than this, that one lay down his life for his friends. You are My friends if you do what I command you. No longer do I call you slaves, for the slave does not know what his master is doing; but I have called you friends, for all things that I have heard from My Father I have made known to you."

John 15:13-15

Lesson Twelve

Control Your Tongue, Part 1

James 3:1-5

Cassandra was known in the church as a leader, a godly woman. She was asked to share devotionals, lead in prayer, disciple younger women, and was involved in a couple of Bible studies. Though she often knew the "right" things to say, Cassandra's tongue could not lie in the more unrehearsed areas of life. When she thought no one was looking, those closest to her knew her inclination to gossip, complain about others, and fight with her husband.

These momentary "slips" of the tongue shone a spotlight on the areas of weakness in her life in ways that even she didn't realize. Those who witnessed this pattern couldn't help but call into question Cassandra's maturity and wisdom. While those who knew her only at church or out in the community respected Cassandra, those who were closest to her saw only a double standard.

Truly our tongue says so much about our credibility and maturity in the faith. While we are not perfect, there should be a pattern of growth in our ability to control our tongue – not only out in the public eye, but more importantly, in our homes, with our loved ones, with those God has given us to especially influence as no other can. May we not grow stagnant, blind, or careless with how we use our tongue, but grow ever more in our ability to be Spirit-led when it comes to our words.

Day One
What Do I See?

1. Describe someone you know who is consistently using their words to honor God and those around them. How do you and others view this person?

> Read James 3:1-5a

James 3:1-5a

¹Let not many of you become teachers, my brethren, knowing that as such we will incur a stricter judgment.
²For we all stumble in many ways. If anyone does not stumble in what he says, he is a perfect man, able to bridle the whole body as well.
³Now if we put the bits into the horses' mouths so that they will obey us, we direct their entire body as well.
⁴Look at the ships also, though they are so great and are driven by strong winds, are still directed by a very small rudder wherever the inclination of the pilot desires.
⁵So also the tongue is a small part of the body, and yet it boasts of great things.

2. Circle the key terms in the passage above. Choose two of the terms to define.

3. Put a box around the objects James uses for illustrations.

4. Underline the command and the warning in this passage.

5. What major comparison is this passage making?

PREPARE YOUR HEART {♥}

6. What result of genuine faith is identified in this passage?

7. What are your initial thoughts about these truths?

8. Be still before the Lord. Ask the Holy Spirit to teach, mature, and guide you this week.

Memory Verse

"For we all stumble in many ways. If anyone does not stumble in what he says, he is a perfect man, able to bridle the whole body as well."

James 3:2

Day Two
A High and Holy Calling

> Read James 3:1-5a

9. What principles can we learn about being a teacher?

10. Look at chapter three in its entirety. What are some reasons James brings up the topic of teaching here?

11. What does it mean to "incur a stricter judgment"? (Consider Luke 12:48 and Hebrews 13:17.)

12. Most of us are not going to be teaching in the specific way that James is writing about. However, we are called to teach in various other ways. What are some of those ways?

13. What conclusions and applications can you draw from this command and warning?

THE EXAMPLE OF GODLY WOMEN

14. Consider the godly women of Proverbs 31 and Titus 2. Fill in the chart below and identify what we can learn from the verses about what and how we are to teach.

SCRIPTURE	WHAT TO TEACH	HOW TO TEACH
Proverbs 31:10-31		
Titus 2:3-5		

Key Term

Perfect: Having reached its end; finished, complete, perfect; fully grown, mature.[1]

15. How are you doing in these specific areas?

Day Three
Maturity: What Would Your Tongue Say?

> Read James 3:1-5a

16. What can you learn about stumbling from this text?

17. What are some areas in which we stumble when it comes to our tongue?

Now pick two or three areas that are a specific struggle to you, and find a verse that can help keep you from stumbling in those areas. Ask the Lord to help you have victory today.

> "Out of the abundance of the heart the mouth speaks."
>
> Matthew 12:34b

18. Recall the definition of "perfect" (see Digging Deeper, Lesson 2). If you are able to control your tongue, what does that reveal about the rest of your life?

DIGGING DEEPER

James mentions the tongue throughout his letter. Summarize what he says in each of these verses: James 1:26; 4:11; and 5:12.

In which of these areas have you seen growth this year? Where does the Lord want you to mature?

Day Four

The Tongue's Direction: Where Are You Headed?

Read James 3:1-5a

19. Record the different objects James uses to illustrate the power of the tongue. Also, note the power that particular object has:

OBJECT	POWER

What conclusions can you draw about the tongue?

12-5

20. **Look up the following passages and share what you find as it relates to the tongue:**

    Psalm 19:14

    Matthew 15:18

    Luke 6:45

The horse and ship in James's illustrations both require the operation of a rider and captain. Depending on who is directing either object will determine its course. According to the above verses, our hearts direct the course of our lives. Who is on the throne of our hearts will greatly affect where our life is headed.

21. **Who is at the "helm" in your life? What do the words of your mouth reveal about the condition of your heart?**

22. **Ask the Lord to help you see how your tongue is directing your life today. Give Him full reign in your heart if there are any areas you have taken over.**

Day Five
STEPPING UP TO MATURITY

Read James 3:1-5a

23. **Find an example in Scripture of someone who controlled their tongue. How did their actions affect others? What did their life reveal about their faith in God? What can you learn from their example?**

Who is on the throne of our hearts will greatly affect where our life is headed.

24. Review what you have learned about *controlling your tongue* this week. Write a principle for living a life of faith based on this passage.

25. What is one thing you can do to become more like the godly woman of Proverbs 31 or Titus 2 as it relates to what was taught in this lesson? What step(s) will you take this week to be a *doer of the Word and not a hearer only* (James 1:22)?

Notes

Lesson Thirteen

Control Your Tongue, Part 2

James 3:5-12

Carol grew up watching *Little House on the Prairie*. She never liked the episode where a young Albert Ingalls and one of his friends snuck a tobacco pipe into the basement of the Blind School during a town picnic. During the episode, the basement door would open unexpectedly and the two boys would throw the lit pipe down on the ground and run quickly up the stairs since they didn't want to get caught. It didn't take long for the embers to ignite into flame. Tragically, the Blind School was burned to the ground, taking the lives of a baby and mother. This was when Carol first saw how destructive fires could be.

This was not the only time that Carol saw the power of fire. It was Christmas the first year of Carol's marriage. She was spending it with her husband's family. A few days before Christmas, a family dinner was served at the dining table. After the meal was cleaned up, the family headed out for some last minute Christmas shopping. Returning to the house after a few hours, her family was greeted with fire trucks, smoke and neighbors gathered outside. Her mind raced back to the *Little House on the Prairie* episode she would always turn off. Thankfully, the house was not burned completely to the ground. The fireman explained that the dining table and Christmas tree had ignited and burned due to a candle that appeared to have been left burning when the family left. Thankfully, most of the damage was due to smoke. The house was covered in black soot, but nothing was hurt beyond repair, and no one was injured.

Those who have had a personal experience with fire can speak of the destructive and lasting damage that occurs. Little else can be as devastating. In the third chapter of James, James chose to use fire as a picture of the damage that can be done by one misspoken word.

Day One
What Do I See?

1. Share a personal experience you or someone you know have had with fire.

Read James 3:5-12

James 3:5-12

⁵So also the tongue is a small part of the body, and yet it boasts of great things. See how great a forest is set aflame by such a small fire!

⁶And the tongue is a fire, the very world of iniquity; the tongue is set among our members as that which defiles the entire body, and sets on fire the course of our life, and is set on fire by hell.

⁷For every species of beasts and birds, of reptiles and creatures of the sea, is tamed and has been tamed by the human race.

⁸But no one can tame the tongue; it is a restless evil and full of deadly poison.

⁹With it we bless our Lord and Father, and with it we curse men, who have been made in the likeness of God;

¹⁰from the same mouth come both blessing and cursing. My brethren, these things ought not to be this way.

¹¹Does a fountain send out from the same opening both fresh and bitter water?

2. Make a list of descriptive words used to describe the tongue.

3. Circle each positive word and draw a wavy line under each negative word. Underline the results the tongue can produce.

   What conclusions can you make from this exercise?

4. Draw a small picture frame next to every illustration James uses. How do these word pictures help explain James's points?

Memory Verse

"So also the tongue is a small part of the body, and yet it boasts of great things. See how great a forest is set aflame by such a small fire!"

James 3:5

PREPARE YOUR HEART {♥}

5. What result of genuine faith is identified in this passage?

6. What are your initial thoughts about these truths?

7. Be still before the Lord. Ask the Holy Spirit to teach, mature, and guide you this week.

Day Two
Power to Destroy

Read James 3:5-12

8. What are some observations you can make about fire and wild animals from verses 5-8? What does the passage actually say about the tongue in regard to these illustrations?

OBSERVATIONS	FIRE	WILD ANIMAL
Basic Truths About Nature		
Actual Statement (vv. 5-8)		

9. How have you seen the tongue used in these ways? What kind of destruction occurred?

10. List some ways to ensure you are not a part of this kind of destruction.

11. James 3:8, in the *New King James* version says, "...no *man* can tame the tongue." If no man can tame the tongue, who can? What does James mean?

"...no man can tame the tongue."

James 3:8 NKJV

13-3

DIGGING DEEPER

Read Galatians 5:19-26 and Colossians 3:5-17. Identify the deeds of the flesh that come by way of the tongue. What help can we find in these passages to become more and more Christ-like in our words?

12. In what ways have you allowed your tongue to be an agent of destruction this past week? Consider whether you need to seek forgiveness from a certain individual, and ask God to help you combat the destructive tendency in your tongue.

Day Three

The Inconsistent Tongue

Read James 3:5-12

13. What are the two main actions James addresses in verses 9-12? Define each using a Bible dictionary or commentary. Who is it directed toward?

ACTIONS	DEFINITIONS	DIRECTED TOWARDS
Blessing		
Cursing		

In which of these areas have you seen growth this year? Where does the Lord want you to mature?

13-4

14. What reasons does James give for his rebuke of their behavior? What others would you add?

15. What are some ways that we "curse" (sometimes without even opening our mouths)? Which do you struggle with the most?

16. How does considering James's reminder that we "have been made in the likeness of God" cause you to stop "cursing" others?

17. Instead of "cursing," what should we be using our mouths for? Consider the following Scriptures:

    Psalm 19:14

    Psalm 35:28

    Psalm 37:30

    Psalm 40:3

18. James again uses the natural world to illustrate his point. When we consider the source of our words, it is not natural for two opposite or contradictory statements to come out of our mouths. In what ways are you guilty of what James is picturing here? Pick one of the above verses to write out and display so that you will see it often and live it out.

19. Ask the Lord to help you praise Him first today from a pure heart and speak words of blessing to those with whom you come in contact.

Proverbs has a great deal to say about the tongue. For extra study, check out the following verses:

Proverbs 10:8, 11, 18-21
Proverbs 11:9
Proverbs 12:22
Proverbs 15:1-2
Proverbs 16:23-24, 27-28
Proverbs 18:7-8, 13

Day Four

From Destruction to Delight: Hannah's Faith

Today we will look at an example of the kind of destruction that can be caused by one woman's tongue, and how another woman blessed God with hers.

20. Read 1 Samuel 1:1-2:10. In the chart below, record what the text says about the two women, their words, and what that reveals about their character:

SUBJECT: WHO WAS SHE?	WORDS	CHARACTER REVEALED
Peninnah		
Hannah		

21. What additional insights can you glean from the interactions between the two women regarding Hannah and her character? What lessons can we learn from Hannah's silence throughout the passage?

22. What help does each of the following verses offer about control of the tongue:

    Psalm 39:1

    Psalm 141:3-4

    Proverbs 26:20

    Ephesians 4:29

    Colossians 4:6

    Hebrews 13:15

    How can these verses help us to be more like Hannah, and less like Peninnah?

    Circle the verse that spoke to you the most and pray about it throughout the week as you are tempted to use unkind words.

"There is one who speaks rashly like the thrusts of a sword, But the tongue of the wise brings healing."

Proverbs 12:18

13-6

Day Five
STEPPING UP TO MATURITY

Read James 3:5-12

23. Find an example from Scripture of a person who had a tongue that destroyed or was inconsistent. How did their actions affect others? What did their life reveal about their faith in God? What can you learn from their example?

24. Is there any area where God has revealed a two-sided heart towards another person or group of people? What will you do this week to change that?

25. Review what you have learned about *the tongue* this week. Write a principle for living a life of faith based on this passage.

26. What step(s) will you take this week to be a *doer of the Word and not a hearer only* (James 1:22)?

Notes

Lesson Fourteen

Exhibit Godly Wisdom

James 3:13-18

Life is like a box of chocolates. Open the box, and there before you is row upon row of the most luscious and delectable little morsels just waiting for your immediate enjoyment. While they are beautiful and alluring on the outside, who knows what you'll ultimately get when you take your first bite. That first one might be your favorite, but the next one might be filled with that orange creme or raspberry goo that seems to be universally despised. How do we know which one to pick? What will we end up with next?

Navigating life can be much like selecting a chocolate from a box. When it comes to wisdom, sometimes what the world has to offer looks just as good on the outside as what God says, until you take that first bite. What looked good and seemed wise at first glance can often leave us disappointed at best, and broken at worst. Like the chocolate, God's wisdom is proven good by what is found on the inside. The heart of God's wisdom can be "tasted" and then "seen" as good.

Just like the chocolate maker includes a map for identifying the inside of each chocolate, so this section in James gives us the code to finding true wisdom. Just like our favorite chocolate is defined by what is inside, so it is with wisdom. God's wisdom is shown by what is in the heart and by the fruit it bears. Who is wise and understanding among you? She is defined by what she is first on the inside. Don't be fooled by the outward appearance. Get a closer look. Choose wisely.

Day One
What Do I See?

1. Who is a wise woman in your life, and what qualities about her make her wise?

> Read James 3:13-18

James 3:13-18

¹³Who among you is wise and understanding? Let him show by his good behavior his deeds in the gentleness of wisdom.
¹⁴But if you have bitter jealousy and selfish ambition in your heart, do not be arrogant and so lie against the truth.
¹⁵This wisdom is not that which comes down from above, but is earthly, natural, demonic.
¹⁶For where jealousy and selfish ambition exist, there is disorder and every evil thing.
¹⁷But the wisdom from above is first pure, then peaceable, gentle, reasonable, full of mercy and good fruits, unwavering, without hypocrisy.
¹⁸And the seed whose fruit is righteousness is sown in peace by those who make peace.

2. List observations found regarding wisdom in verses 14-15. What title would you give this section?

   List observations found regarding wisdom in verses 13, 17-18. How would you title this section?

3. What is being contrasted in these two sections?

4. What "fruit" is born of each type of wisdom?

5. Record the question posed (verse 13), and write the answer in your own words.

Memory Verse

"But the wisdom from above is first pure, then peaceable, gentle, reasonable, full of mercy and good fruits, unwavering, without hypocrisy."

James 3:17

PREPARE YOUR HEART {♥}

6. What result of genuine faith is identified in this passage?

7. What are your initial thoughts about these truths?

8. Be still before the Lord. Ask the Holy Spirit to teach, mature, and guide you this week.

Day Two
Wisdom Is Seen, Not Just Heard

THE QUESTION POSED: WHO IS WISE?

> Read James 3:13-18

9. Using a Bible dictionary, define the terms "wise" and "understanding."

10. What qualities would the world use to answer James's question (verse 13)?

11. What attributes does James use to answer his question in verse 13?

12. What are some other words for "gentleness" (consider looking it up in a Bible dictionary)?

How is gentleness a key ingredient to godly wisdom?

Notes

13. Think of a recent situation that required wisdom. Share what part gentleness played in the scenario, and whether things could have been different with or without it.

14. Record what the following Scriptures say with regard to wisdom:

    Psalm 111:10

    1 Corinthians 1:18-2:16

    James 1:5

    How do your answers above highlight what is important to God when it comes to wisdom?

15. How do the qualities you value regarding wisdom match up with what God values? How are they evident in your life?

Day Three
Worldly Wisdom

> Read James 3:13-18

WORLDLY WISDOM'S MOTIVATION

16. The motives of worldly wisdom are identified in verse 14, "in your heart." Our heart will dictate how we act. What does James say will be in the heart as it relates to worldly wisdom?

17. How do the terms James uses describe the "wisdom" we find in our society around us? How would you describe that person?

18. Is it possible for a believer to act in their own way? In what ways do we see this in the church?

"Watch over your heart with all diligence, For from it flow the springs of life."

Proverbs 4:23

19. **Take a moment and evaluate how you are doing in these areas. How are you personally doing in regard to jealousy, comparing/competing, promoting self or things for yourself, pride, etc.? Take a minute to write a prayer in response to these thoughts.**

WORLDLY WISDOM'S CHARACTERISTICS

20. **Describe the three characteristics of worldly wisdom found in verse 15:**

    Earthly:

    Natural:

    Demonic:

WORLDLY WISDOM'S RESULTS

21. **What are the results of worldly wisdom?**

John MacArthur writes, "Both **disorder** and **every evil thing** are obviously broad terms that cover a multitude of specific bad results... **[Disorder]** has the basic meaning of instability, and hence came to be used of a state of confusion, disturbance, disarray, or tumult... **Every evil thing** is the broadest possible category of the bad results produced by human wisdom. In its better sense, ...**[evil]** means worthless; in its worst, it means vile and contemptible."[1]

22. **What are some real life examples that we can find in the world today?**

> "Every good thing given and every perfect gift is from above, coming down from the Father of lights, with whom there is no variation or shifting shadow."
>
> James 1:17

23. **The wisdom of this world has a way of weighing us down. Think of the people you are interacting with, the decisions you are making, and the counsel you are giving or seeking. What kind of impact does this type of wisdom have on those around us, our personal relationships, the church, and our interactions with the unsaved?**

24. **How can you guard yourself against acting on the wisdom of the world?**

Day Four
Wisdom from Above

> Read James 3:13-18

25. **In what areas do women need to be wise?**

In verse 17, James illustrates how true wisdom looks; a welcome change from our lesson yesterday. If the wisdom of the world is motivated by a desire to gratify self first, then godly wisdom is motivated by a desire to please God first. When a woman is living with that desire in the center of her heart, the qualities James speaks of will be evident in her life.

26. **Next to each characteristic of godly wisdom, list ways you would see those demonstrated in the life of a believer:**

Pure - free from defilement, blemish, contamination - speaks of motives. Ways *purity* is demonstrated in a believer's life:

Peaceable - a peacemaker, not stirring up conflict or divisive; not forcing own opinion, but working for peace. Ways *peace* is demonstrated in a believer's life:

Gentle - equitable, seemly, fair, moderate, forbearing, courteous, considerate; humbly patient; coming alongside, meek, humble. Ways *gentleness* is demonstrated in a believer's life:

"Do not love the world nor the things in the world. If anyone loves the world, the love of the Father is not in him. For all that is in the world, the lust of the flesh and the lust of the eyes and the boastful pride of life, is not from the Father, but is from the world. The world is passing away, and also its lusts; but the one who does the will of God lives forever."

1 John 2:15-17

Reasonable - *willing to yield without rancor or disputing; teachable, compliant, not stubborn; willing submission (as to a military commander).* Ways *reasonableness* is demonstrated in a believer's life:

Full of Mercy - *forgiving, compassionate, reaching out, caring for suffering persons.* **[Full of] Good Fruits** - *good deeds, fruit of the Spirit.* Ways *mercy* is demonstrated in a believer's life:

Unwavering - *not to be parted or divided - without uncertainty, indecision, inconsistency, vacillation, doubtfulness; impartial, treats everyone equally, without favoritism; without hypocrisy.* Ways *unwavering* is demonstrated in a believer's life:

JESUS' LIFE OF FAITH

27. Pick two of the characteristics of godly wisdom and find an example of how Jesus exhibited those.

    How does this motivate you to follow His example in a situation you need wisdom in right now?

RESULTS OF GODLY WISDOM

28. What are the results from this type of godly wisdom (verse 18)? How is it sown and by whom?

29. Consider your life, your marriage, your relationship with your kids, your coworkers, and friends. How would those relationships be enhanced if your interactions were guided by this type of wisdom? What might be different? Ask the Lord to fill your heart with a desire to know Him, His Word and live in His wisdom.

Notes

Day Five
STEPPING UP TO MATURITY

Read James 3:13-18

DIGGING DEEPER

We can't live out what we do not know. However, we can gain knowledge without living it out. Are we merely storing up knowledge (puffs up) or are we using what we are learning in our everyday life? Look at the following Scriptures and note the importance of God's Word in your life:

Deuteronomy 6:1-9

Ezra 7:10

Psalm 1:1-3

Psalm 119:11

John 8:31

2 Timothy 2:15

2 Timothy 3:16-17

Notes

30. Find another place in Scripture where you can gain additional insight into the value of godly wisdom. What did you learn from this passage?

31. Review what you have learned about *wisdom* this week. Write a principle for living a life of faith based on this passage.

32. What step(s) will you take this week to be a *doer of the Word and not a hearer only* (James 1:22)?

Notes

Lesson Fifteen

Have a Heart Focused on God

James 4:1-5

Sarah had decided that the next time the weekly ads came out, she was going to go shopping and buy some new boots. The latest style had come out and she felt behind. Even though she'd been watching and her favorite store hadn't even gotten them in yet, she knew that several ladies in her church would most likely be wearing those same boots soon. She wanted to be the trend-setter. She didn't really care if there wasn't quite enough money in the budget. She had to have those boots! Maybe she could pray that God would provide an extra assignment at work. Perhaps a few extra hours would cover the cost of the boots.

As she was thinking about this, Sarah was startled when she realized she was in church and should have been listening to pastor's message. Her Bible study leader had advised the gals in her group that the sermon was going to be pertinent to the lesson the next week. Sarah didn't want to miss the chance to give a correct answer. The sermon was on something she wasn't really interested in, but she tried to pay attention. The lady in front made it a little hard to concentrate. She must have forgotten to do her hair that morning. Who cares if she has twin babies! This is church, after all! Certainly she could have brushed her hair.

On the way home, Sarah decided she needed to call her friend Mona. They'd had an argument over some silly decorations for the next ladies luncheon and Sarah thought she'd give Mona a chance to apologize. Sarah was sure she was right and certainly Mona could see that by now. Sarah had wondered why their relationship was so strained lately. Being a single gal, Sarah treasured the relationships she had with her friends, and things hadn't been the same between them lately. She should pray about that, too. Jesus did pray for unity between believers, after all.

In this story, Sarah's heart was longing after things that had earthly value, and little heavenly importance. She was distracted from things that had eternal impact. Sarah was experiencing little peace and joy in her relationship with her Savior, and her relationship with her friend was strained.

In James 4, we see a congregation who was experiencing very little peace and joy in their relationship with God, and their interactions with one another were strained, at best. Scripture is filled with God's desire for us to have a pure heart and relationship with Him. God knows that when we seek Him in purity, we will be fulfilled and will be filled with peace and joy. An indication of our close relationship with Him is that we are at peace with those around us.

Day One
What Do I See?

1. This week, what were the simple things that God did that reminded you of His love?

> Read James 4:1-5

James 4:1-5

¹What is the source of quarrels and conflicts among you? Is not the source your pleasures that wage war in your members?
²You lust and do not have; so you commit murder. You are envious and cannot obtain; so you fight and quarrel. You do not have because you do not ask.
³You ask and do not receive, because you ask with wrong motives, so that you may spend it on your pleasures.
⁴You adulteresses, do you not know that friendship with the world is hostility toward God? Therefore whoever wishes to be a friend of the world makes himself an enemy of God.

2. **In the passage above, James uses several cause and effect phrases. Mark the cause and effect phrases by underlining both phrases and draw an arrow from the cause to the effect.**

3. **Also from the passage above, circle the struggles and conflicts of these believers.**

4. **What specific word in this passage shows that these believers have a relationship with God?**

PREPARE YOUR HEART {♥}

5. What result of genuine faith is identified in this passage?

6. What are your thoughts about these truths?

7. Be still before the Lord. Ask the Holy Spirit to teach, mature, and guide you this week.

Memory Verse

"You adulteresses, do you not know that friendship with the world is hostility toward God? Therefore whoever wishes to be a friend of the world makes himself an enemy of God."

James 4:4

Day Two

War Within: My Response to God

> Read James 4:1-5

8. Referring back to the cause and effect phrases in Day One, what was at the heart of the conflicts with which these believers were struggling?

9. In the believers' relationship with God, what areas were impacted by these conflicts?

10. Explain the significance of James's choice of the word "adulteresses."

11. In our culture today, what worldly things do you see yourself, or others, longing after?

12. List some ways that these longings put us in opposition toward God.

13. In what ways do you see longing for worldly things affecting your relationship with God?

14. "Or do you think that the Scripture says in vain, 'The Spirit who dwells in us yearns jealously'?" (James 4:5, NKJV). What do you think this verse means?

"For those who are according to the flesh set their minds on the things of the flesh, but those who are according to the Spirit, the things of the Spirit. For the mind set on the flesh is death, but the mind set on the Spirit is life and peace, because the mind set on the flesh is hostile toward God; for it does not subject itself to the law of God, for it is not even able to do so,..."

Romans 8:5-7

Day Three

War Within: My Response to Others

> Read James 4:1-5

15. Describe the interactions of believers in James 4.

16. Chart God's desires for our relationships and interactions with other believers.

VERSE	GOD'S DESIRES...
John 13:34	
John 17:22-23	
Galatians 5:13	
1 Peter 1:22	

17. What important steps would one need to take in order to follow God's desires?

18. How would following after God and His desires impact our own life and church?

Key Term

Adulteress: "James's way of addressing (and with shock value!) those who are spiritually unfaithful to God, those who are making pleasure the chief end of life."

DIGGING DEEPER

Read John 14:21; Matthew 22:37; and Colossians 3:1-14. What can you learn about...

God?

God's desire for us?

God's desire for our relationships with others?

Day Four
Barnabas' Faith

Read Acts 4:32-5:11

19. List the characteristics of the body of Christ displayed in the church at Jerusalem.

20. Contrast the atmosphere of this congregation to that as found in James 4.

21. There are two examples of believers found in the Acts passage. First, what did Barnabas' offering reveal?

Notes

22. **For the second example of believers, fill in the chart below with your observations about Ananias and Sapphira.**

Their physical condition:
Their heart condition:
The interaction between Peter and Ananias:
The interaction between Peter and Sapphira:

23. **What was the impact of Ananias' and Sapphira's sin on themselves?**

24. **List ways in which we choose death over life when following our selfish desires.**

25. **Sapphira was offered a chance to choose life! Describe a time when you were offered a second chance. What was the result of that choice?**

Day Five
STEPPING UP TO MATURITY

> Read James 4:1-12

26. Find an example in Scripture of a person whose heart was not focused on God. How did their actions affect others? What did their life reveal about their faith in God? What can you learn from their example?

27. Examine your heart and ask God to reveal any areas of worldliness that separate you from a deeper relationship with Him. Instead of filling your needs with worldliness, ask God to show you how to fill your need with Him.

28. Review what you have learned about *having a heart focused on God* this week. Based on James 4:1-12, write a principle for living a life of faith.

29. What step(s) will you take this week to be a *doer of the Word and not a hearer only* (James 1:22)?

Notes

Lesson Sixteen

Have a Humble Heart

James 4:6-10

Throughout her college career, Katherine had been a student leader in the local Christian college club and had also been discipling several different freshman girls over the past year. She would be coming back from summer vacation ready to finish out her last year and graduate with a Bachelor's Degree in Counseling. At the beginning of the summer, Katherine had been pleased with the way her relationships with her mentees left off. She had finished a successful year helping them navigate through hard relationships, homesickness, tough class schedules, even divorce. However, as the year had progressed, Katherine felt more and more empty. She would pray, but felt distant from the Lord. She couldn't figure out why life had all of a sudden become more complicated.

At the 4th of July picnic, Katherine happened into her old Sunday School teacher, Mrs. Kimball. Katherine found herself sharing her troubles. In talking with Mrs. Kimball, Katherine soon realized that she had slowly begun putting faith in her own abilities as a counselor more than in God's ability to meet the needs of her mentees. This pride in herself had caused her to turn just slightly away from God. The turning away compounded itself until she found herself distanced. Katherine asked God's forgiveness for her pride and over the next few weeks committed to spend time in God's Word. She found herself filled with peace, joy, and gratefulness. She returned to school ready to follow God wherever He led, knowing that He would provide everything that she needed in order to accomplish His will.

Katherine came to see how her pride drove a wedge into her relationship with the Lord. She sought to remove her pride, and found peace and joy once again in her relationship with God. In James 4:5-10, we see God's stance on pride and grace and the effect both have on our relationship with Him. God gives us clear direction on how to put aside our pride and what needs to happen in our hearts in order to be right with God.

Day One
What Do I See?

1. Think about someone who demonstrates humility in their life. Describe their actions/attitudes.

Read James 4:6-10

James 4:6-10

⁶But He gives a greater grace. Therefore it says, "GOD IS OPPOSED TO THE PROUD, BUT GIVES GRACE TO THE HUMBLE."
⁷Submit therefore to God. Resist the devil and he will flee from you.
⁸Draw near to God and He will draw near to you. Cleanse your hands, you sinners; and purify your hearts, you double-minded.
⁹Be miserable and mourn and weep; let your laughter be turned into mourning and your joy to gloom.
¹⁰Humble yourselves in the presence of the Lord, and He will exalt you.

2. Why were these believers to be miserable, mourning, and weeping?

3. What enemy is identified in the passage?

4. What actions are identified in this passage?

PREPARE YOUR HEART {♥}

5. What result of genuine faith is identified in this passage?

6. What are your thoughts about these truths?

7. Be still before the Lord. Ask the Holy Spirit to teach, mature, and guide you this week.

Memory Verse

"But He gives a greater grace. Therefore it says, 'GOD IS OPPOSED TO THE PROUD, BUT GIVES GRACE TO THE HUMBLE.' Submit therefore to God. Resist the devil and he will flee from you."

James 4:6-7

Day Two
God Is Opposed to the Proud...

> Read James 4:6-10

8. What can you learn about pride from the following passages?

   Proverbs 8:13

   Proverbs 16:5

   Proverbs 29:23

   1 John 2:16

9. Based on your study, write your own definition of "pride."

10. How does this pride separate us from God?

11. What does this pride cost us?

12. In what areas of your life do you struggle with pride? What might pride be costing you?

"Do not grieve the Holy Spirit of God, by whom you were sealed for the day of redemption."

Ephesians 4:30

DIGGING DEEPER

Do a word study on being thankful. How would a thankful heart contribute to maintaining a humble heart?

Day Three

...But [God] Gives Grace to the Humble

Read James 4:6-10

James 4:1-5 describes believers who are preoccupied by worldly desires and therefore, are called double-minded and enemies of God. James 4:7-10 is God's prescription for believers who have been convinced of their sin, have chosen to turn from their sin, and are ready to live for Christ.

13. List the commands James gives for drawing near to God and turning away from worldliness in verses 7-10.

14. How are you doing in following God's commands?

15. According to James 4:6, 8, and 10, how does God assist us?

16. What evidences should we look for in a life submitted to God?

"Then Jesus said to His disciples, 'If anyone wishes to come after Me, he must deny himself, and take up his cross and follow Me.'"

Matthew 16:24

17. Read Philippians 2:5-11. Summarize how Jesus was an example to us of humility.

18. Write a brief prayer of thanksgiving to your amazing Savior for being such an example of humility and obedience.

Day Four
Paul's Faith

Paul took great pride in his Jewish heritage and accomplishments. Once he was saved, Paul no longer considered these things of any consequence compared to the value of knowing Jesus Christ as Savior. Paul was a good example of one who turned from the praises of men in order to follow Christ.

> Read Acts 9:1-21; Galatians 1:13-14; Philippians 3:3-11

19. What was the state of Paul's heart and relationship with God before his conversion?

20. List the "qualifications" that gave him reason to be proud.

21. What changes took place during and after his encounter with God?

22. How does Paul's testimony of God's grace encourage you in your faith in the sufficiency of God's grace and in your battle against pride?

Notes

Day Five

STEPPING UP TO MATURITY

> Read James 4:1-12

23. Find an example in Scripture of a person who humbly sought after God. How did their actions affect others? What did their life reveal about their faith in God? What can you learn from their example?

24. Review what you have learned about a *humble heart*. Write a principle for living a life of faith based on this passage.

25. What step(s) will you take this week to be a *doer of the Word and not a hearer only* (James 1:22)?

Notes

Lesson Seventeen

Give Grace

James 4:11-12

Martha's son had an upcoming eighth grade field trip to the coast. She was at the last meeting when he came up and begged her to come along. They needed another female chaperone. After considering her to-do list, she decided she'd be able to put some things off for a time and went ahead and committed to go.

Days later, as the group piled onto the bus, Martha's jaw dropped as she spotted Julie, one of the other moms. She had seen Julie many times at other school events over the last few years, and had often wanted to get to know her. Julie had always impressed Martha as one of those "fashionable" moms with her cute haircut and expensive clothes. She looked as if she worked at a high-powered job. Over the next few days, they chatted while the kids ran around learning about history on the coast. Martha found that her impression of Julie was quite different than reality. Julie was a mom with a son who was autistic. She was very generous with her time and resources, even donating her hair to charity every few years – which accounted for her fashionable short haircut.

Martha realized that only a few short years ago, she would have judged Julie based on her appearance and because she wasn't a Christian. She would have missed out on the friendship that had developed. However, over the last few years, Martha had learned that judging went against God's desires for her. Martha was so grateful that God had been working in her heart. Instead of missing an opportunity, she was already looking forward to the chance to share Christ with Julie.

Martha had made judgments about Julie, when in reality, Julie turned out to be much different. As Christians who long to honor our Savior but still struggle against our human flesh, we can look to Scripture for help in this area. James speaks directly to those who struggle with judging and speaking against others.

Day One
What Do I See?

1. What kind of contest would you like to judge? Why?

> Read James 4:11-12

James 4:11-12

¹¹Do not speak against one another, brethren. He who speaks against a brother or judges his brother, speaks against the law and judges the law; but if you judge the law, you are not a doer of the law but a judge of it.
¹²There is only one Lawgiver and Judge, the One who is able to save and to destroy; but who are you who judge your neighbor?

2. Circle the key words in this passage and define them.

3. Underline the commands in this passage.

4. Put a box around words referring to God.

5. What is only God able to do?

6. List the actions of the believers identified in this passage.

PREPARE YOUR HEART {♥}

7. What result of genuine faith is identified in this passage?

8. What are your initial thoughts about these truths?

9. Be still before the Lord. Ask the Holy Spirit to teach, mature, and guide you this week.

Memory Verse

"Do not speak against one another, brethren. He who speaks against a brother or judges his brother, speaks against the law and judges the law; but if you judge the law, you are not a doer of the law but a judge of it. There is only one Lawgiver and Judge, the One who is able to save and to destroy; but who are you who judge your neighbor?"

James 4:11-12

Day Two

The Heart Condition and the Result

> Read James 4:11-12

10. The quality of our relationship with others reflects the quality of our relationship with God. What is at the heart of one who speaks against or judges others?

11. Look at the definitions of "speak against" or "judging" to the side. Compare and contrast the terms.

12. Read John 8:44. The devil in this passage literally means "slanderer or accuser of the brethren." What insights does this add to the seriousness of "speaking against others"?

13. Record what you learn about judging from these passages:

    Romans 2:1-5

    Romans 14:10-19

    Ephesians 4:17-25

14. What are the results of judging others?

15. In what ways do believers struggle with:

    Speaking against others?

    Judging?

    Where do you personally struggle in these areas?

16. According to James 4:6, God provides a grace that is greater! Take a moment to thank the Lord for the grace He gives to us.

Key Terms

Speak against: "Speaking about others behind their backs in a derogatory manner ... It reflects backbiting, faultfinding and harsh criticism." [1]

Judging: "To judge someone entails what goes on in our heart and mind. This judging would be harsh and would include judging one's motives and conducts." [2]

"If someone says, 'I love God,' and hates his brother, he is a liar; for the one who does not love his brother whom he has seen, cannot love God whom he has not seen."

I John 4:20

Day Three
God's Desire for Unity

Read James 4:11-12

When we slander or judge others, we sin, we bring judgment on ourselves, and we cause disunity among believers. Jesus talked about unity as He prayed with His disciples at the Last Supper. Paul teaches about love and unity in his letters.

17. Record God's desire for believers. What would be the opposite of His desire? Record these answers as well.

VERSE	GOD'S DESIRE	OPPOSITE OF GOD'S DESIRE
John 17:17-23		
1 Corinthians 13:4-7		
Ephesians 4:1-4		
Colossians 3:12-15		

18. Look at the column of "opposites." How does this reflect a judgmental heart?

19. What results could you expect in your relationships if judgmental hearts were replaced with God's desires?

20. How can this impact you personally, the church, and the world?

"Beyond all these things put on love, which is the perfect bond of unity."

Colossians 3:14

DIGGING DEEPER

Find another place in Scripture where you can gain additional insight into the unity of believers. What did you learn from this passage? Be prepared to share with your group.

Day Four

Jesus' Life of Faith

Read John 8:2-11

21. Make some basic observations about this scene.

22. What were the Pharisees hoping for? What was Jesus' response?

23. What do the actions of the Pharisees reveal about their attitude toward the adulterous woman? Themselves?

24. In light of James 4:12, what does Jesus' response to the woman teach us about God as Lawgiver and Judge?

25. Based on Jesus' response, how should we respond to others?

26. Compare the impact the Pharisees had on the woman's life with Jesus' impact.

27. In what ways does Jesus' example encourage you when you are tempted to judge others?

17-5

Day Five

STEPPING UP TO MATURITY

Read James 4:1-12

28. Find an example in Scripture of a person who spoke out against others, or judged others. How did their actions affect others? What did their life reveal about their faith in God? What can you learn from their example?

29. Examine your heart and ask God to reveal any areas of judgmentalism that separate you from a deeper relationship with Him. Ask God to give you a heart for people that is like His own.

30. Review what you have learned about *speaking against or judging others*. Write a principle for living a life of faith based on this passage.

31. What step(s) will you take this week to be a *doer of the Word and not a hearer only* (James 1:22)?

Notes

Lesson Eighteen

Trust God's Will

James 4:13-17

One day in Disneyland was all that was in the plan for the Smith's family vacation, and they had determined it was going to be a good day. The weather of course would be perfect, the crowds wouldn't be that bad, and the kids ... well, they would get along. The day had been planned perfectly. With a schedule in hand for each of the rides downloaded from a computer program, their first task was to get to the park by 9 a.m. in order to be boarding the first ride at 9:10 a.m.

The first glitch came before they even arrived. Stopping for an iced mocha on the way put them behind schedule on their perfectly planned out day. The GPS said they wouldn't arrive until 9 a.m. and then there would be parking to find, shuttles to ride and tickets to buy. Not to mention the traffic in LA that still needed to be navigated.

Arriving later than intended, the Smith family ran to the first ride and then the second trying to make up for lost time. Sticking to the plan was a priority for the day. The dark clouds loomed in the sky. Umbrellas certainly were not included in the plan. With the printed schedule wet from the rain, and stuffed in their pocket, they proceeded.

Are you a planner? Do you make your list and love to check things off? Do you dream about your future and all that will happen? There is nothing wrong with careful planning, but James has a few suggestions for the heart of every planner.

Day One
What Do I See?

1. What do you enjoy planning (vacations, events, your future, etc.)?

> Read James 4:13-17

James 4:13-17

¹³Come now, you who say, "Today or tomorrow we will go to such and such a city, and spend a year there and engage in business and make a profit."
¹⁴Yet you do not know what your life will be like tomorrow. You are just a vapor that appears for a little while and then vanishes away.
¹⁵Instead, you ought to say, "If the Lord wills, we will live and also do this or that."
¹⁶But as it is, you boast in your arrogance; all such boasting is evil.
¹⁷Therefore, to one who knows the right thing to do and does not do it, to him it is sin.

2. Circle who James is talking to in this passage.

3. Underline all the words that have to do with time in the above passage.

4. Write the two quotations contrasted in this passage in your own words:

   1._____
   2._____
   Which one do you find yourself saying (or something similar) most often?

PREPARE YOUR HEART {♥}

5. What result of genuine faith is identified in this passage?

6. What are your initial thoughts about these truths?

7. Be still before the Lord. Ask the Holy Spirit to teach, mature, and guide you this week.

Memory Verse

"Yet you do not know what your life will be like tomorrow. You are just a vapor that appears for a little while and then vanishes away. Instead you ought to say, 'If the Lord wills, we will live and also do this or that.'"

James 4:14-15

Day Two

Our Plans vs. God's Will

> Read James 4:13-17

8. List the plans laid out in verse 13.

9. What is the motivation of the person making these plans?

10. What does James object to in their planning?

> Read Luke 12:16-21

11. What insights can you gain from this parable about planning? What specifically was God's reply?

12. Have you been guilty of leaving God out of your plans? What happened?

"As for the days of our life, they contain seventy years, Or if due to strength, eighty years, Yet their pride is but labor and sorrow; For soon it is gone and we fly away. Who understands the power of Your anger And Your fury, according to the fear that is due You? So teach us to number our days, That we may present to You a heart of wisdom."

Psalm 90:10-12

Day Three

Disobedience of God's Will

> Read James 4:13-17

13. In verse 16, James addresses boasting. How would boasting get in the way of God's will?

14. Use verse 17 to define sin in your own words.

    How does 2 Peter 2:21 enrich your answer?

15. In what ways can our planning become sin?

16. Verse 17 can also apply to all areas in the Christian life. Look back at the other lessons you have learned in James. Are you applying them? When might you be one who knows to do the right thing and does not do it? Take time to evaluate this in your life.

> *"'If it is the Lord's will,' ought to infect our thinking."*
>
> Elizabeth George

Day Four
Living in God's Will

"James is not against making plans ... he is not taking a cheap shot at charts or making an argument against commitments ... What James warns us about is that our freedom to make plans is not a license to live free from God. To come to that conclusion would be arrogant ... The phrase, 'If it is the Lord's will,' ought to infect our thinking. It ought to be a standard part of our vocabulary."[1]

Read James 4:13-17

17. What instructions are given in regard to careful planning (verse 15)?

18. Fill your name in the verse:
    "Instead, _____ ought to say, 'If the Lord wills, _____ will live and also do this or that.'"

19. It is not just about the exact phrasing, but about the attitude of the heart. In what ways will you incorporate these instructions as you make plans and live in God's will?

PAUL'S FAITH

20. How did Paul address his plans in the following passages?

   Acts 18:21

   Romans 1:10

   1 Corinthians 4:19

   1 Corinthians 16:7

   How do these verses show Paul's attitude of faith?

21. What area of your life needs to demonstrate this type of faith?

DIGGING DEEPER

Find two Proverbs that encourage careful planning. What truths did you learn?

Day Five
STEPPING UP TO MATURITY

> Read James 4:13-17

22. Find an example in Scripture of a person who trusted God's will for their plans. How did their actions affect others? What did their life reveal about their faith in God? What can you learn from their example?

23. What future plans are you making? Have you spent time asking God for His will in your planning? Ask your group for prayer in this area.

24. Review what you have learned about God's will in the area of *planning* this week. Write a principle for living a life of faith based on this passage.

25. What step(s) will you take this week to be a *doer of the Word and not a hearer only* (James 1:22)?

Notes

Lesson Nineteen

Use Riches in a Godly Way

James 5:1-6

Have you ever had a pet hamster? I don't recommend it. They only cost about ten bucks, but they'll suck you dry with all the stuff that you just have to have in order to provide an adorably comfy habitat. I don't think any of us knows how a hamster might live in the wild, so we give ours a clear plastic condominium with a tube connecting to a guest house, a second tube connecting to a home gym and a vertical tube leading to the vista house. We furnish the compound with a bed, a feeding center (gotta have choices), the aforementioned exercise equipment, and toys it will never use. Sometimes we take it out on a field trip in an exercise ball.

I don't think a hamster even knows how a hamster would survive in the wild. But that is where pet store people found them, right? Are there still pods or herds or gaggles of hamsters being wrangled somewhere in Guatemala? The long-awaited point here is that hamsters hoard everything they can find, and store it in the comfy little nest you made them—the equivalent of a single bed. There isn't any space for piles of stuff. It's just a place to sleep. But your little hamster, in its palatial estate, has insisted on bringing everything it considers of value into the one place you have designated for it to find rest. It just stuffs those cheeks until its face is wider than its body is long.

It doesn't need to forage every last morsel and hide it under the bed. You have given it plenty, and you will do it again tomorrow. When it's time to clean the cage, you find the majority of the hoard ruined by hair, sawdust chips, and other unmentionable contaminants. You're going to remove that and have to throw it away. The hamster doesn't know or trust that more provision will come, even though you have never left it wanting. It's every rodent for himself. There's no wonder they prefer to live alone. They don't want to share. They want more than they need, and will collect it to the point of destruction. Poor little rich oppressor. The hamster doesn't even know how to be happy with everything it has. It wouldn't share if given the opportunity. Let's get a bunny.

How often are we prone to act in a similar way when it comes to what God has lavished upon us in terms of riches? James delivers a strong exhortation to the rich oppressors concerning their treatment of other believers and the misuse of their riches. The message is clear ... consequences will come. We have a tremendous opportunity to bring glory to His name by the way we use our riches—either worldly or eternally.

Day One
What Do I See?

1. If you were to inherit a substantial sum of money within the next week, how would you choose to use it?

> Read James 5:1-6

James 5:1-6

¹Come now, you rich, weep and howl for your miseries which are coming upon you.
²Your riches have rotted and your garments have become moth-eaten.
³Your gold and your silver have rusted; and their rust will be a witness against you and will consume your flesh like fire. It is in the last days that you have stored up your treasure!
⁴Behold, the pay of the laborers who mowed your fields, and which has been withheld by you, cries out against you; and the outcry of those who did the harvesting has reached the ears of the Lord of Sabaoth.
⁵You have lived luxuriously on the earth and led a life of wanton pleasure; you have fattened your hearts in a day of slaughter.
⁶You have condemned and put to death the righteous man; he does not resist you.

2. What problem is James addressing in this passage?

3. Underline the warnings James has for those with a wrong view of money.

4. Circle the way the rich man lived.

PREPARE YOUR HEART {♥}

5. What result of genuine faith is identified in this passage?

6. What are your initial thoughts about these truths?

7. **Be still before the Lord. Ask the Holy Spirit to teach, mature, and guide you this week.**

Memory Verse

"Therefore, to one who knows the right thing to do and does not do it, to him it is sin."

James 4:17

Day Two
Worldly Perspective or Eternal Perspective?

> Read James 5:1-6

As we move our way into James 5:1-6, we read again the key phrase "Come now..." Recall in James 4:13-17, that James was chastising the brethren concerning the plans they were making without consulting the Lord. James continues his chastisement concerning these rich oppressors using their money for their own desires ... in very ungodly ways.

8. **What specific points did James want these rich oppressors to understand?**

9. **What types of possessions does the rich man have (verses 2-3, 5)?**

   How does this expose his heart?

Instructions to rich believers are found in 1 Timothy 6:17-19. There is a stark contrast between having a worldly perspective or having an eternal perspective regarding the wealth we have on earth.

> Read 1 Timothy 6:17-19

10. **In James 5:1-6, what were the rich oppressors fixing their hope on?**

    What instructions are laid out for us in 1 Timothy?

    How does this encourage you?

11. **In light of 1 Timothy 6:17-19, how are you using your riches to invest eternally?**

"This poor man cried, and the Lord heard him And saved him out of all his troubles."

Psalm 34:6

12. Matthew 6:19-21 tells us, "Do not store up for yourselves treasures on earth, where moth and rust destroy, and where thieves break in and steal. But store up for yourselves treasures in heaven, where neither moth nor rust destroys, and where thieves do not break in or steal; for where your treasure is, there your heart will be also." Prayerfully consider where your "treasure is stored." Ask God to reveal to you any areas that might need changing when it comes to using your riches to glorify Him.

Day Three

Warning: Do Not Hoard Your Riches!

> Read James 5:1-6

In James 5:4, we see another example of how the rich oppressors' misuse of their money demonstrated their character. They were hoarders.

13. Look up the word "hoard" in a dictionary and write a definition in your own words.

14. Read Job 29:12-17. In the chart below, note the contrasts between the rich oppressors in James 5:4 and Job in Job 29:12-17.

RICH OPPRESSORS James 5:4	JOB Job 29:12-17

15. To protect laborers from oppressive employers, the Law contained precise instructions concerning their pay. Read Leviticus 19:13; Deuteronomy 24:14-15; and Jeremiah 22:13. Record your observations below.

"These rich men had hired the laborers and promised to pay them a specific amount. The men had completed their work but had not been paid. The tense of the verb 'kept back' (withheld) in the original Greek indicates that the laborers never will get their salaries." [1]

16. Although we are no longer under the Law, how do these instructions relate to us today?

17. Consider ways that you might be "hoarding" your riches. Ask the Lord to reveal to you areas of potential change.

DIGGING DEEPER

The rich oppressors and their treatment of the poor is an ongoing theme in the book of James. Remember James 2:6, "...Is it not the rich who oppress you and personally drag you into court?" "Oppress" in this verse literally means "to tyrannize." James again states the fact that God is fully aware of the rich oppressors' treatment of the poor – the treatment that includes condemnation and even death (verse 6).

God's name in James 5:4 is "the Lord of Sabaoth." Using a Bible dictionary or commentary, research the meaning of this name. What insight does this give into the passage?

Day Four
A Poor Widow's Faith

Read James 5:1-6

Read the short account of the poor widow found in Mark 12:41-44.

18. Picture the scene, observing the people and the money they are depositing into the treasury. What distinct differences do you notice about what the rich people and the poor widow put into the treasury? What does that say about their heart?

Notes

19. What does Jesus say about the poor widow's giving (verse 43)?

20. What specific lesson(s) was Jesus desiring to teach His disciples and teach us today?

21. Notice in verse 44 that Jesus states twice that she gave her all. What does sacrificial giving mean to you?

22. Does the amount of giving look the same for everyone? Use 2 Corinthians 8:12; 9:6-15 to support your answer.

23. It is evident that the poor widow understood the meaning of sacrificial giving and using her riches in a godly way. Examine your own heart to determine if this is true in your own life. Ask God to reveal to you any areas that need changing.

Day Five

STEPPING UP TO MATURITY

Read James 5:1-6

24. Find an example in Scripture of a person who used their riches in a godly way. How did their actions affect others? What did their life reveal about their faith in God? What can you learn from their example?

Notes

25. Review what you have learned about *using your riches in a godly way* this week. Write a principle for living a life of faith based on this passage.

26. What step(s) will you take this week to be a *doer of the Word and not a hearer only* (James 1:22)?

Notes

Lesson Twenty

Display Patient Endurance in the Midst of Suffering

James 5:7-12

Camping. A favorite pastime for millions of Americans. It's not mine, but my whole family loves it, and I am a team player. Secretly (or perhaps not), I think it's a mild form of suffering. Camping comes with all the things that a modern woman is not fond of. The pain starts days before you leave. Everything you need in your comfy home on a daily basis, you will need to pack and haul for your five day "vacation."

Clothes for every season will need to be packed, because, if not previously implied, you will be outside THE ENTIRE TIME. Yeah, a tent doesn't count as indoors. Mornings are cold, possibly foggy. Afternoons are most likely warm, and by dinner it might be unbearably hot. Never fear though, evening s'mores by the campfire will hearken the return of the cold that you get to try to sleep in. Count 'em. Three clothing changes. In one day. Per person. Now back to trying to sleep. You will share your tent with all of the insects that laugh in the face of zippers as a home security system. And since you're on the ground, you're extra vulnerable to crawling things.

Oh, good morning. Did you sleep well? The bathrooms are down the hall, well, the path, to the right about five sites down, and since you were freezing all night, and you already have thirty mosquito bites, and you can't take a shower in the river today, it's probably your time of the month too. Oh yeah, you better go back to camp and bring your own soap. This is a state campground. Embrace nature. They have no soap.

It's time to make breakfast. Good luck opening the bear locker that has all of your food in it. Good luck finding a toy in your cereal instead of an actual spider. Good luck lighting your camping stove to make pan toast and scrambled eggs after that spider came tumbling out of your Honey Nut Cheerios. Oh hey, don't turn the burner off yet. You have to heat water and wash your dishes. The water spigot is down the hall, uh path, about two sites down. You should have seen it on your way back from the bathroom.

I'm kidding, of course. Camping's awesome. Don't worry. It'll be fun. Just make sure you go with another family so that you can borrow their soap when you realize you forgot yours. That's probably what started my downhill spiral in the first place. Yeah, it was the soap. Camping's fun...

It is very easy to laugh at this comical display of so called "suffering." But what about those deep, dark times when the end to our suffering seems nowhere in sight? James offers hope and encouragement in this passage with the gentle reminder that we are to patiently endure whatever affliction God allows in our lives. "The LORD'S lovingkindnesses indeed never cease, For His compassions never fail. They are new every morning; Great is Your faithfulness. 'The LORD is my portion,' says my soul, 'Therefore I have hope in Him.'" Lamentations 3:22-24

Day One
What Do I See?

1. What kind of camping (or other outdoor) "suffering" have you experienced?

> Read James 5:7-12

James 5:7-12

⁷Therefore, be patient, brethren, until the coming of the Lord. The farmer waits for the precious produce of the soil, being patient about it, until it gets the early and late rains.

⁸You too be patient; strengthen your hearts, for the coming of the Lord is near.

⁹Do not complain, brethren, against one another, so that you yourselves may not be judged; behold, the Judge is standing right at the door.

¹⁰As an example, brethren, of suffering and patience, take the prophets who spoke in the name of the Lord.

¹¹We count those blessed who endured. You have heard of the endurance of Job and have seen the outcome of the Lord's dealings, that the Lord is full of compassion and is merciful.

¹²But above all, my brethren, do not swear, either by heaven or by earth or with any other oath; but your yes is to be yes, and your no, no, so that you may not fall under judgment.

2. **Circle the key words in this passage.**

3. **Underline any repeated key phrases.**

4. **Make a list of commands in this passage.**

PREPARE YOUR HEART {♥}

5. What result of genuine faith is identified in this passage?

6. What are your initial thoughts about these truths?

7. Be still before the Lord. Ask the Holy Spirit to teach, mature, and guide you this week.

Memory Verse

"You too be patient; strengthen your hearts, for the coming of the Lord is near."

James 5:8

Day Two
Be Steadfast!

> Read James 5:7-12

Verses 7-8 are just as applicable today as they were the day James wrote them. As you have already observed, the obvious command is for these suffering believers to be patient – to strengthen their hearts; this is the exhortation. The encouragement? Be steadfast! There is good purpose for this suffering and His timing is perfect! The coming of the Lord is near!

8. The "coming of the Lord" is repeated twice in these two verses. What does this truth refer to in relation to this passage?

    What hope does this bring as you patiently endure suffering?

9. Why is it difficult for you to remain steadfast and to trust His timing during suffering?

10. Refer to the definition in the side bar. What are some ways that you "strengthen your heart"?

11. Many passages in God's Word encourage us as they speak of God's purpose in our suffering. Fill in the chart with the encouragement you gain from these passages.

2 Corinthians 1:3-5	
Hebrews 13:5b-6	
1 Peter 1:6-7	

As you have already observed, the obvious command is for these suffering believers to be patient to strengthen their hearts; this is the exhortation.

Key Term

Strengthen your hearts: To make fast, to establish, to confirm ... from the root word that means "to cause to stand" or "prop up."

12. **How can remembering these truths encourage you in the midst of suffering?**

13. **We understand God's perfect timing when it comes to seasons and weather, but we don't always understand His timing and ways in our own lives. Reflect on the season of life you are in right now. Are you able to fully grasp God's good purpose and perfect timing concerning the suffering He allows in your life? Why or why not?**

Ask Him to help you view your suffering from His perspective. "For I am confident of this very thing, that He who began a good work in you will perfect it until the day of Christ Jesus." Philippians 1:6

Day Three
Job's Faith

> Read James 5:7-12

"This is the only place in the New Testament where Job's name is mentioned ... Using Job as an example, James is saying to look not at circumstances, but look at the end. See the big picture."[1]

14. **Read Job 1:1-2:10 and write a summary of the suffering Job faced.**

15. **In the chart below, record your observations concerning how Job responded to this suffering.**

Job 1:20-22	
Job 19:25-26	
Job 23:10-12	
Job 42:1-2	

Notes

16. What encouragement comes with actually "seeing" Job's response?

Although it is important to note the tangible blessings Job received (Job 42:12), there is much, much more to the blessings gained while enduring tremendous suffering. As James 5:11 reminds us, "...the Lord is full of compassion and is merciful."

17. Describe a time when you patiently endured during a season of suffering and experienced God's compassion and mercy.

What abundant intangible blessings did you experience?

Job 42:5 says, "I have heard of You by the hearing of the ear; but now my eye sees You..." We can't choose our suffering, but we can be thankful because suffering allows us to know God in a way we wouldn't have, had we not experienced it. That's part of the blessing. Our lives are changed and our growth is evident because of the goodness of God. As you endure hardship and suffering, ask the Lord to help you clearly "see" the abundant blessings. May you be able to say, "I have tasted and I have seen that the Lord is good (Psalm 34:8)!"

DIGGING DEEPER

Jonah, Hosea, Daniel and Jeremiah are just some of the examples of those suffering prophets referred to in James 5:10. Choose an example of a suffering prophet. Tell how they endured and what you can learn from their example.

Notes

Day Four
Our Response Matters

| Read James 5:7-12 |

What a fitting example James uses to encourage believers to display patient endurance in the midst of suffering! Like Job, we have plenty of opportunity to complain about our circumstances, our family and our friends. We need to consider the fact that **our responses to suffering matter.** We must not allow our circumstances to dictate our responses.

DO NOT COMPLAIN

The word "complain" in verse 9 means "a sigh or to groan." This carries the idea that actual words may not even come from the mouth, but sounds of groaning, sighing, murmuring, or grumbling. This is oftentimes no more apparent than in our own homes, directed toward our own loved ones.

18. **In relation to complaining, what is your typical response when you are subjected to suffering of any kind?**

19. **What do these responses reveal about you?**

20. **Consider the following verses to be reminded of what your response should be when enduring any kind of hardship.**

REFERENCE	PROPER RESPONSE
Psalm 5:1-3	
1 Thessalonians 5:16-18	
James 1:2-5	

DO NOT SWEAR

When we are in the midst of especially difficult times, it is easy to say things we do not mean and make promises to God we do not have the ability to keep. James encourages believers to let their "yes" be "yes" and their "no" be "no" (verse 12).

Key Term

Swear: ..."to affirm or deny something by an oath."

21. In terms of making promises to the Lord, what is your typical response when subjected to suffering of any kind?

22. What do your promises to God reveal about how you view Him?

23. Consider a current hardship you are experiencing. Based on these verses, what will you do to endure it with patience?

Day Five
STEPPING UP TO MATURITY

Read James 5:7-12

24. Find an example in Scripture of a person who displayed patient endurance in the midst of suffering. How did their actions affect others? What did their life reveal about their faith in God? What can you learn from their example?

25. Review what you have learned about *displaying patience in the midst of suffering* this week. Write a principle for living a life of faith based on this passage.

26. What step(s) will you take this week to be a *doer of the Word and not a hearer only* (James 1:22)?

"...Making oaths or vows were not forbidden but rather encouraged ... The act of making a vow was acceptable. The acts of breaking a vow or making rash vows were condemned."[2]

Lesson Twenty-One

Pray Earnestly and Effectively

James 5:13-20

Jenny was finally pregnant with her first child. She and Scott had been waiting on God's timing for this blessing for eight years. Their son had been named since a newly-engaged Jenny had started envisioning domestic bliss, over ten years earlier. But as Scott's dad was diagnosed with cancer during the second trimester, and would not live to see his grandson, they were both moved to name this baby after his grandfather. Scott was able to whisper the secret to his father the day before he died. At that point, even the baby's gender had been a secret to everyone else on earth. Because his dad had lost the ability to speak in his final days, Jenny and Scott relished the thought of him making the big announcement to the hosts of heaven upon his arrival.

The pregnancy had gone smoothly for almost seven months, when Jenny woke up with a burning ache somewhere in her abdomen. Thinking it might be her gall bladder, her doctor (who was away) advised her to go to the emergency room if she still had pain when Scott came home from work. Forty-eight hours and two ambulance transports later, Jenny was greeted in her hospital room with a parade of doctors, nurses, surgeons, and anesthesiologists, each taking turns telling her their own version of the same scary story. She was going to have this baby in a matter of days, not months.

William Richard made his entrance three days later, ungreeted by either parent, as Jenny had been anesthetized due to the severity of her condition, and Scott was kept out of the room as a precaution. His weight would later be debated among the O.R. staff, but he was a dinky three pounds and some change and ready for a fight. He would get one five days later, when in an emergency abdominal surgery, his appendix was found to be ruptured. Immediately, Jenny and Scott enlisted family and friends to pray and pass on the request. A mighty army of prayer warriors from their church and beyond arose in the days to follow, and then went to their knees on behalf of little Will. He was God's Will, Jenny and Scott began calling him, because that was who held him in His hands. Given no other choice in this new role of parenting, that gave them peace. They prayed that God would do HIS will with theirs. God saw to it, because of the prayers of the people and because He is sovereign, to baffle the medical community by empowering His little Will to overcome a 4 percent chance of survival.

That boy is a testament every day, to every man, woman, and child who was blessed to participate in those prayers, that God is sovereign and He hears us when we cry to Him. And to this day, that healthy, amazing, giant boy is still called God's will.

How important is prayer offered in faith? Consider the possible outcome of Scott and Jenny's journey had they not enlisted the prayers of these saints on behalf of "God's Will." James alludes to the potential our prayers have and the enormity that can be accomplished if we offer prayers in faith. We are called to pray earnestly in any and all circumstances, with faith, believing that God will answer according to His will.

Day One

1. Have you ever prayed for something over an extended period of time? In what ways did you see God answer?

> Read James 5:13-20

James 5:13-18

¹³Is anyone among you suffering? Then he must pray. Is anyone cheerful? He is to sing praises.

¹⁴Is anyone among you sick? Then he must call for the elders of the church and they are to pray over him, anointing him with oil in the name of the Lord;

¹⁵and the prayer offered in faith will restore the one who is sick, and the Lord will raise him up, and if he has committed sins, they will be forgiven him.

¹⁶Therefore, confess your sins to one another, and pray for one another so that you may be healed. The effective prayer of a righteous man can accomplish much.

¹⁷Elijah was a man with a nature like ours, and he prayed earnestly that it would not rain, and it did not rain on the earth for three years and six months.

¹⁸Then he prayed again, and the sky poured rain and the eaerth produced its fruit.

2. What major themes do you notice presented in this passage?

3. Underline the commands found in this passage.

4. What is being compared in verse 17?

PREPARE YOUR HEART {♥}

5. What result of genuine fatih is identified in this passage?

6. What are your initial thoughts about these truths?

7. Be still before the Lord. Ask the Holy Spirit to teach, mature, and guide you this week.

Memory Verse

"Therefore, confess your sins to one another, and pray for one another so that you may be healed. The effective prayer of a righteous man can accomplish much."

James 5:16

Day Two
Prayer Offered in Faith Brings Promise

Read James 5:13-20

Both of the words "sick" found in these verses mean "to be weary, feeble or weak." This passage is not necessarily referring to physical sickness, but more likely to a spiritual condition of weariness, weakness or feebleness. This weariness can be a result of more than one reason. Suffering through a trial can lead to a weakened state spiritually or physically. The text also speaks to the fact that this weakened state could be a result of sin.

8. According to verses 13-14, how should a believer respond if they find themselves in a weakened state spiritually or physically?

9. Fill in the chart to understand what kind of prayer God desires if the "sickness" is due to sin.

REFERENCE	RESPONSE
Psalm 32:5	
Proverbs 28:13	
1 John 1:9	

10. If our "sickness" is due to sin, God's desire is that our prayers would be prayers of confession. How does confession affect future prayers?

DIGGING DEEPER

Research the meaning of "anointing him with oil" as seen in James 5:14. Tell the significance of this and if it is applicable to us today.

Suffering? Pray!
Psalm 50:15
Psalm 91:15
Psalm 107:6
Zechariah 13:9

Cheerful? Sing praises!
Job 35:10
1 Corinthians 14:15
Ephesians 5:18-19
Colossians 3:16

<u>Misconception</u> James 5:15 says, "...and the prayer offered in faith will restore the one who is sick..." Often times this is taken out of context and taught incorrectly: "If the elders, or those who are praying, <u>just have enough faith</u>, this person will be made well physically." What if this person is not made well? Has God failed in His promise? No! A person may be called home due to sickness. This is not a result of lacking faith, as some choose to teach in a condemning way.

11. In what ways are the elders to pray? Why is this significant?
    (c.f. John 14:13-14; 1 John 5:14-15)

12. What are the promises resulting from these prayers (verse 15)?

13. What encouragement does this bring you when you consider how the elders are to pray for you?

14. We are encouraged to pray no matter the state we find ourselves in, and we can expect that God will answer according to His will. Prayers of faith bring hope and promise. As you reflect on your life, describe a time when you experienced the promises of God's truth. Share with your group the impact this experience had on you.

Day Three
Be Accountable!

Read James 5:13-20

15. What are the clear commands in verse 16?

16. Refer to the list of the righteous man's qualities found in the side bar. What significance do these qualities have in terms of accountability?

An elder is regarded as a spiritual leader within the church and his role is of considerable importance in the life a believer.

Acts 20:28; Titus 1:7; 1 Peter 5:1-2

Key Terms

Restored: (or saved) means to save, deliver or protect, heal, to be made whole.

Raised up: to waken, to rouse – from sleep, from sitting/lying, from disease, from death, from obscurity.

Forgiven: forsake, lay aside, omit, send away.

Righteous Man: yields to the Spirit; submits to God's Word; sensitive to sin; quick to confess and seek forgiveness from God and others wronged; obedient; trusts the Lord.

17. There are instructions in Scripture that speak to this idea of accountability. Match the following instructions with the references:

   Restore with gentleness   a. Matthew 18:15
   Bear one another's burdens   b. 2 Corinthians 2:7
   Forgive and comfort   c. Galatians 6:1
   Admonish   d. Galatians 6:2
   Confront privately   e. 1 Thessalonians 5:11
   Encourage one another   f. 2 Thessalonians 3:15

18. What are some reasons individuals may not seek out accountability?

19. What benefits come when believers have regular accountability with other Christians?

20. There is tremendous power and potential when individuals meet together for prayer and accountability. Prayerfully consider that this may be something God would have you be involved in and earnestly pray about who He would have you be accountable to. If you are involved in accountability, take a moment to share with your group how it has impacted you.

Day Four
Elijah's Faith

James 5:13-20

21. Read Deuteronomy 28:1-2, 15 in the sidebar. What specific reasons did God give for punishing the nation of Israel with 3 1/2 years of drought?

"Now it shall be, if you will diligently obey the Lord your God, being careful to do all His commandments which I command you today, the Lord your God will set you high above all the nations of the earth. All these blessings shall come upon you and overtake you if you obey the Lord your God … But it shall come about, if you will not obey the Lord your God, to observe to do all His commandments and His statutes with which I charge you today, that all these curses shall come upon you and overtake you."

Deuteronomy 28:1-2, 15

22. Read 1 Kings 17-18. Sprinkled throughout this narrative are examples of Elijah's prayers of faith. Although we don't read Elijah's prayers in this account concerning the drought, we are able to see many outcomes of his effective prayers. List the outcomes you have observed in these two chapters.

23. Read 1 Kings 18:36-46 again and notice the confidence with which Elijah prays at the time of the offering of the evening sacrifice and the demonstration that was to follow. What was the outcome of this demonstration (verse 39)? How does this encourage you?

24. What contrast do you notice between Ahab and Elijah in verses 41 and 42? Why is this significant?

25. Verse 42 says, "...and he crouched down on the earth and put his face between his knees." In what ways does this posture display Elijah as a "righteous man"?

26. "Then he prayed again, and the sky poured rain..." (James 5:18). How was his prayer answered? What does this show you about the way God answers prayer?

27. Elijah's prayers were not necessarily effective and powerful because of his position as a prophet, but because his relationship with the Lord directed his desires and requests. Because he knew the heart of God, he prayed in faith according to God's will. What example can you use from Elijah to improve your prayer life?

Notes

Day Five
STEPPING UP TO MATURITY

> Read James 5:13-20

28. Find an example in Scripture of a person who prayed earnestly and effectively. How did their actions affect others? What did their life reveal about their faith in God? What can you learn from their example?

29. Review what you have learned about *praying earnestly and effectively* this week. Write a principle for living a life of faith based on this passage.

30. What step(s) will you take this week to be a *doer of the Word and not a hearer only* (James 1:22)?

Notes

Lesson Twenty-Two

A Final Evaluation

It seemed like yesterday when Shelby first walked the halls of the University as a freshman. Time had flown by. It wouldn't be long and she would make her final walk down the aisle to receive her diploma. Her dream to teach English as a second language in Bangladesh was soon to become a reality. Upon completion of graduation, she would be heading to the airport for the long flight over the Atlantic.

Packing was a bit of a challenge. She had so much she wanted to take with her, but limited space. All the books she had accumulated over the last four years had become bittersweet friends. As much as she wanted to take them with her, she knew she would have to leave most behind. As she carefully folded her clothes, Shelby couldn't help but wonder if she was really prepared for this new adventure. Would she be able to remember what she had learned within the walls of her classrooms? Was she ready to switch roles and become the teacher instead of the student?

Sifting through papers from the past four years she stumbled across an "Entry Test" she had taken during her Freshman Seminar class. It was a required test given to all freshmen to assess their basic knowledge as they entered college. As she sat down on the bare floor, she took a moment to review. She giggled to herself over some of the answers she had given back then. Wow, she really had learned a lot over the past four years. Yet some of the questions she had missed back then still stumped her. Feelings of accomplishment mingled with recognition that there was still much to learn and many areas in which she needed to continue to grow. Shelby slowly put the test aside as she tucked one last book in her suitcase. Yes, she could be a teacher, but she would always be a student. She determined right then she would continue her pursuit of learning and growing; she would never be done. There would always be more to learn and always be areas in which her mind could expand. After all, being a learner herself would make her a better teacher for her students.

As we wrap up our lessons in James and the qualities of faith, we find ourselves in much the same place as Shelby; thankful for all that we have learned, and yet eager to continue to grow. God has refined our faith, clarifying its qualities, and He will continue that good work in us!

Day One
Evaluating Faith

1. How has a woman of faith impacted your faith?

After many weeks of examining different qualities of faith, take time now to prayerfully review and reflect on each quality.

2. Read the entire book of James. Refer back to the title you gave the book of James in Lesson 1, #3 on page 1-2. Would you change the original title? Why or why not? If so, what would you change it to?

PREPARE YOUR HEART {♥}

3. As you review the qualities of faith that are revealed in James, what is your response to what you have learned?

4. Be still before the Lord. Ask the Holy Spirit to teach, mature, and guide you this week as you review each quality of faith.

Day Two
Rejoice in Trials

5. Read James 1:1-12. Describe the quality of faith: "rejoices in trials."

Memory Verse

"Even so faith, if it has no works, is dead, being by itself. But someone may well say, 'You have faith and I have works; show me your faith without the works, and I will show you my faith by my works.'"

James 2:17-18

6. What evidence do you see in your life of faith that "rejoices in trials"?

7. What steps do you desire to take to continue to grow in this area?

Do Not Blame God

8. Read James 1:13-16. Describe the quality of faith: "does not blame God."

9. What evidence do you see in your life of faith that "does not blame God"?

10. What steps do you desire to take to continue to grow in this area?

Respond Correctly to God's Perfect Gifts

11. Read James 1:17-18. Describe the quality of faith: "responds correctly to God's perfect gifts."

Notes

12. What evidence do you see in your life of faith that "responds correctly to God's perfect gifts"?

13. What steps do you desire to take to continue to grow in this area?

Respond Correctly to God's Word

14. Read James 1:19-27. Describe the quality of faith: "responds correctly to God's Word."

15. What evidence do you see in your life of faith that "responds correctly to God's Word"?

16. What steps do you desire to take to continue to grow in this area?

Do Not Show Favoritism

17. Read James 2:1-13. Describe the quality of faith: "does not show favoritism."

18. What evidence do you see in your life of faith that "does not show favoritism"?

Notes

19. What steps do you desire to take to continue to grow in this area?

Day Three
Show Faith Through Works

20. Read James 2:14-20. Describe the quality of faith: "shows faith through works."

21. What evidence do you see in your life of faith that "shows faith through works"?

22. What steps do you desire to take to continue to grow in this area?

Take Action

23. Read James 2:21-26. Describe the quality of faith: "takes action."

24. What evidence do you see in your life of faith that "takes action"?

25. What steps do you desire to take to continue to grow in this area?

Notes

Control Your Tongue

26. Read James 3:1-12. Describe the quality of faith: "controls the tongue."

27. What evidence do you see in your life of faith that "controls the tongue"?

28. What steps do you desire to take to continue to grow in this area?

Exhibit Godly Wisdom

29. Read James 3:13-18. Describe the quality of faith: "exhibits godly wisdom."

30. What evidence do you see in your life of faith that "exhibits godly wisdom"?

31. What steps do you desire to take to continue to grow in this area?

Have a Heart Focused on God

32. Read James 4:1-4. Describe the quality of faith: "has a heart focused on God."

Notes

33. What evidence do you see in your life of faith that "has a heart that focuses on God"?

34. What steps do you desire to take to continue to grow in this area?

Have a Humble Heart

35. Read James 4:5-10. Describe the quality of faith: "has a humble heart."

36. What evidence do you see in your life of faith that "has a humble heart"?

37. What steps do you desire to take to continue to grow in this area?

Day Four
Give Grace

38. Read James 4:11-12. Describe the quality of faith: "gives grace."

Notes

39. What evidence do you see in your life of faith that "gives grace"?

40. What steps do you desire to take to continue to grow in this area?

Trust God's Will

41. Read James 4:13-17. Describe the quality of faith: "trusts God's will."

42. What evidence do you see in your life of faith that "trusts God's will"?

43. What steps do you desire to take to continue to grow in this area?

Use Riches in a Godly Way

44. Read James 5:1-6. Describe the quality of faith: "uses riches in a godly way."

Notes

45. What evidence do you see in your life of faith that "uses riches in a godly way"?

46. What steps do you desire to take to continue to grow in this area?

Display Patient Endurance in the Midst of Suffering

47. Read James 5:7-12. Describe the quality of faith: "displays patient endurance in the midst of suffering."

48. What evidence do you see in your life of faith that "displays patient endurance in the midst of suffering"?

49. What steps do you desire to take to continue to grow in this area?

Pray Earnestly and Effectively

50. Read James 5:13-20. Describe the quality of faith: "prays earnestly and effectively."

51. What evidence do you see in your life of faith that "prays earnestly and effectively"?

52. What steps do you desire to take to continue to grow in this area?

Notes

Day Five
STEPPING UP TO MATURITY

53. Reflect on all that you have learned through studying the book of James and God's description of the qualities of faith. What has impacted you the most?

54. Write out a prayer thanking God for all He has done, and ask Him to continue His good work in your life.

Notes

Notes

James, Maturing in Faith

Lesson 1
   1. Vine, W. E. Vines Expository Dictionary of Biblical Words. Nashville: Thomas Nelson, 1996.

Lesson 2
   1. Nystrom, David P. NIV Application Commentary. Grand Rapids: Zondervan, 1997.
   2. Hughes, Phillip E. The New International Commentary on the New Testament. Grand Rapids: Eerdmans Pub. Co, 1962.

Lesson 4
   1. Lenski, RCH. The Interpretation to the Epistle of the Hebrews and the Epistle of James. USA: Augsburg Fortress Publishers, 2008
   2. Bruckner, James. NIV Application Commentary; Habakkuk. Grand Rapids: Zondervan, 2004.

Lesson 7
   1. Strauss, Lehman. James Your Brother. New York: Loizeaux Brothers, 1956.

Lesson 9
   1. The Nelson Study Bible. Nashville: Thomas Nelson, 2008.

Lesson 11
   1. Swindoll, Charles. Abraham the Friend of God. Insights for Living Press. Frisco, 1988.

Lesson 12
   1. Vine, W. E. Vines Expository Dictionary of Biblical Words. Nashville: Thomas Nelson, 1996

Lesson 14
   1. MacArthur, John. The MacArthur new Testament Commentaries: James. Chicago. 1998

Lesson 15
   1. George, Elizabeth. Growing in Wisdom and Faith. Eugene: Harvest House, 2001

Lesson 17
   1. Heck, Susan. With the Master in the School of Tested Faith. Mustang: Tate Publishers, 2006.
   2. Heck, Susan. With the Master in the School of Tested Faith. Mustang: Tate Publishers, 2006.

Lesson 18
   1. George, Elizabeth. Growing in Wisdom and Faith. Eugene: Harvest House, 2001.

Lesson 19
   1. Wiersbe, Warren. Be Mature. Colorado Springs: David C. Cook, 2008.

Lesson 20
   1. Heck, Susan. With the Master in the School of Tested Faith. Mustang: Tate Publishers, 2006.
   2. Heck, Susan. With the Master in the School of Tested Faith. Mustang: Tate Publishers, 2006.

Made in the USA
Lexington, KY
02 January 2018